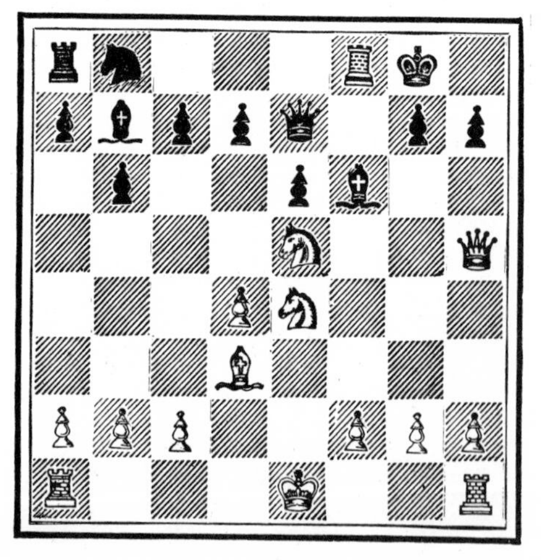

White checkmates in eight moves. (See page 55.)

CHESS AND CHECKERS

THE WAY TO MASTERSHIP

BY

EDWARD LASKER

COMPLETE INSTRUCTIONS FOR THE BEGINNER
VALUABLE SUGGESTIONS FOR THE ADVANCED PLAYER

THIRD REVISED EDITION

DOVER PUBLICATIONS, INC.
NEW YORK NEW YORK

Published in Canada by General Publishing Company, Ltd., 30 Lesmill Road, Don Mills, Toronto, Ontario.
Published in the United Kingdom by Constable and Company, Ltd., 10 Orange Street, London WC 2.

This Dover edition, first published in 1960, is a revised version of the work originally published by D. Appleton & Co. in 1918.

Standard Book Number: 486-20657-2
Library of Congress Catalog Card Number: 60-16349

Manufactured in the United States of America
Dover Publications, Inc.
180 Varick Street
New York, N. Y. 10014

PREFACE

A quadratic board of 64 squares, two opposing groups of pieces with names suggesting military maneuvers and court intrigue, a few rules governing the moves of these pieces in their efforts to checkmate the hostile king—and you have the one game which, coming out of dim antiquity, has outlasted all world empires, survived all political and social revolutions.

Chess exerts a fascination which knows no difference in age or occupation. The philosopher and the mathematician, the musician and the artist, the diplomat and the actor, the business man and the working man—you find them all among the hundred thousands of the game's loyal fans.

The strategic implications of the struggle on the Chess board, naturally, always made the game especially attractive to the military mind.

Frederick the Great, Napoleon and Moltke, the great scientists of war, had a decided liking for Chess and quite likely owed to it many an inspiration which helped them in laying out their military plans. Indeed, no other game exists which offers such complete analogies to war.

Two armies oppose each other on the Chess board, composed of different units which may well be compared with infantry, cavalry and artillery. The success of the operations on the board, which represents the battlefield, does not depend upon any element of chance, but solely upon the ingenuity and the skill of the players who are the commanders-in-chief of the forces.

Although a Chess game differs from a battle in that the material strength of the opponents is equal, the order of events is the same in Chess as in war. The troops are first mobilized and made ready for action with utmost speed, then important positions are occupied which give the troops freedom of action and insure safe lines of retreat and, finally, when the formation of the enemy is known, the strategic plan is made which the generals try to carry out by means of different tactical maneuvers.

If Chess cultivates strategic ability, it certainly trains other qualities of the mind which are useful in our daily practical life.

The faculty which is developed by playing Chess is useful wherever logical thinking and concentration are needed, and it cannot be denied that these qualities are most desirable in the every day struggle in which mental work has so largely superseded manual labor.

The thoughtful playing of the game not only cultivates the logical quality and imaginative power of the mind but also tends to develop strength of character. It teaches us not to be hasty in our decisions, but to exercise foresight at all times as we must abide by all consequences of our actions. Moreover, we learn from it circumspection which causes us to survey the whole scene of action and does not allow us to lose ourselves in detail; we also learn not to be discouraged by reverses in our affairs but to hold out and always search for fresh resources.

Thus, Chess serves a good purpose for young and old. The boy will find it a fascinating pastime and, unconsciously sharpening his wits in playing the game, will acquire a fine preparation for his calling in life, no matter what it may be. For the man, and the woman too, Chess is well worth learning, as it will prove the best companion in hours of leisure.

The reason why many people hesitate to learn the game and to teach it to their children is that Chess has been misrepresented as a game which is very difficult to master. This false impression has been created mainly by the wrong methods of teaching usually employed. The majority of writers on Chess deal with a maze of variations and they expect the reader to memorize the moves with which to parry the maneuvers of the opponent, instead of simply developing a few common sense principles which are easy to grasp and perfectly sufficient to make a good player of any one.

This is really the great advantage of the game of Chess over any other board game, that it lends itself to the application of general principles, so that any one can grasp and enjoy it without memorizing more than the rules according to which the men move.

I have tried to develop these principles in a simple way so that they are sure to be easily understood, and I have been greatly aided in my task by Miss Helen Dvorak and Mr. Eugene Fuller, who, without any previous knowledge of the game, have learned it in reading through the manuscript of this book. They have given me many valuable hints in pointing out all that did not seem readily intelligible to the mind of the beginner.

In explaining the game of Checkers, to which the second part of the book is devoted, I have also tried to develop general principles of strategy, rather than to offer a mere classification of analyzed lines of play, which the reader would have to memorize in order to be able to compete with experts.

I was fortunate enough to secure the collaboration of the Checker Champion, Alfred Jordan, who enthusiastically adopted the new idea of teaching and furnished most of the material which I have used in illustrating the vital points of the game.

EDWARD LASKER

INTRODUCTION

THE HISTORY OF CHESS

The game of Chess in the form in which it is played to-day is usually assumed to be of a much older date than can be proved with certainty by documents in our possession. The earliest reference to the game is contained in a Persian romance written about 600 A.D., which ascribes the origin of Chess to India. Many of the European Chess terms used in the Middle Ages which can be traced back to the Indian language also tend to prove that India is the mother country of the game.

We are, therefore, fairly safe in assuming that Chess is about 1300 years old. Of course we could go farther, considering that the Indian Chess must have been gradually developed from simpler board games. Indeed we know from a discovery in an Egyptian tomb built about 4000 B.C. that board games have been played as early as 6000 years ago; but we have no way of finding out their rules.

The game of Chess spread from India to Persia, Arabia and other Moslem countries, and it was brought to Europe at the time of the Moorish invasion of Spain. It also reached the far East, and games similar to Chess still exist in Japan, China, Central and Northern Asia, the names and rules of which prove that they descended from the old Indian Chess.

In Europe Chess spread from Spain northward to France, Germany, England, Scandinavia and Iceland. It became known with extraordinary rapidity, although at first it was confined to the upper classes, the courts of the kings and the nobility. In the course of time, when the dominance of the nobility declined and the inhabitants of the cities assumed the leading rôle in the life of the people, the game of Chess spread to all classes of society and soon reached a popularity which no other game has ever equaled.

While in the early Middle Ages the game was played in Europe with the same rules as in the Orient, some innovations were introduced by the European players in the later Middle Ages which proved to be so great an improvement that within a hundred years they were generally adopted in all countries including the Orient. The reason for the changes was that in the old form of the game it took too long to get through the opening period. The new form, which dates from about 1500 A.D. and the characteristic feature of which is the enlarged power of Queen and Bishop, is our modern Chess, the rules of which are uniform throughout the civilized world.

In the Seventeenth Century Chess flourished mostly in Italy, which consequently produced the strongest players. Some of them traveled throughout Europe, challenging the best players of the other countries and for the most part emerging victorious. At that time Chess was in high esteem, especially at the courts of the kings who received traveling masters with open arms and rewarded them liberally for their exhibition matches.

Towards the beginning of the Eighteenth Century the game reached a high stage of development in France, England and Germany. The most famous master of the time was the Frenchman, André Philidor, who for more than forty years easily maintained his supremacy over all players with whom he came in contact, and whose fame has since been equaled only by the American Champion, Paul Morphy, the German, Emanuel Lasker, the Cuban, José Raoul Capablanca, and the Russian, Alexander Alexandrovich Alekhine.

During the Eighteenth and Nineteenth Centuries the number of players who obtained international fame increased rapidly, and in 1851, due to the efforts of the English Champion Staunton, an international tournament was held in London to determine the championship of Europe. It was won by the German master Anderssen, who maintained his leading place for the following fifteen years, until he was beaten by the youthful Morphy. The latter, at twenty years of age, was the first American master to visit Europe and defeated in brilliant style all European masters whom he met.

Morphy withdrew from the game after his return to America and did not try to match himself with the Bohemian Steinitz, who in the meantime had beaten Anderssen, too, and who had come to America.

Steinitz assumed the title of the World's Champion and defended it successfully against all competitors until 1894, when he was beaten by Emanuel Lasker, mathematician and philosopher, who held the title for twenty-seven years. He was finally defeated by Capablanca, at Havana in 1921. The Cuban, who had been considered unbeatable by his fellow masters, lost his crown to Alekhine in 1927 at Buenos Aires, in a memorable match which lasted several months due to the fact that 25 of the 34 games played ended in a draw. When Alekhine died in 1946, he was still in possession of the World title, having lost it to Max Euwe of Amsterdam in 1935 but regained it in a return match in 1937.

The International Chess Federation (FIDE) decided to determine Alekhine's successor to the Chess throne by a tournament in which the six players who were generally considered the strongest masters of the world competed. The contest was won by the Russian Mikhail Botvinnik. Every three years a similar tournament takes place, the winner of which forthwith challenges the champion. Up to now all challengers have been Soviet players: David Bronstein, Vassily Smyslov, Mikhail Tal, Tigran Petrosian and Boris Spassky. There are only two or three Americans of comparable caliber. The Soviet players are at a great advantage due to the fact that Chess has become their national game, enlisting millions of fans every year who engage in a thorough analysis of the openings. The knowledge of these analyses has accounted for a good many victories of Soviet masters over adversaries unfamiliar with them.

Ever since the beginning of this century the leading Chess Clubs of the different countries arranged, as an annual feature, national and international tournaments, thus bringing the Chess players of all nationalities into close contact.

This internationalism of Chess is of great advantage to the Chess player who happens to be traveling in a foreign country. There are innumerable Chess Clubs spread all over the globe and the knowledge of the game is the only introduction a man needs to be hospitably received and to form desirable social and business connections.

It would be going beyond the limit of this summary of the history of Chess if I tried to give even an outline of the extremely interesting part Chess has played in French, English and German literature from the Middle Ages up to the present time. Suffice it to mention that Chess literature by far exceeds that of all other games combined. More than five thousand volumes on Chess have been written, and weekly or monthly magazines solely devoted to Chess are published in all countries, so that Chess has, so to speak, become an international, universal language.

HISTORY OF CHECKERS

The literature on the game of Checkers (English: Draughts) is very limited and there are no certain references to prove that the game was known before the Sixteenth Century. Two theories are current as to its origin; one of them claiming it to be a simplified Chess, the other explaining it as the result of transferring the Spanish game *Alquerque de doze* to the Chess board.

H. J. R. Murray, the greatest authority on the history of games, considers it most likely that the game has been evolved from both Chess and Alquerque. The method of capturing men and the rule concerning the *huffing* of a man unquestionably point to the Spanish game, while the board, the diagonal move of the men and the idea of crowning a man are taken from Chess.

In France, Germany, Italy and Spain the name of the game is still that of the Queen of Chess (Dame, Dama) whose move in the Middle Ages was identical with the move of the Checkermen.

Checkers has never been able to attain more than national uniformity, and it is played with different rules in different countries. In the United States it is more popular than in any other country and a number of players have obtained national fame.

CONTENTS

PART II

PART I

THE GAME OF CHESS

I

THE RULES OF THE GAME

BOARD AND MEN

The game of Chess is played by two armies who oppose each other on a square board or battlefield of sixty-four alternate white and black squares. Each army has sixteen men; one King, one Queen, two Rooks (or Castles), two Bishops, two Knights and eight Pawns. The Generals of the two armies are the two players themselves. The men of one side are of light color and are called White, those of the other side are of dark color and are called Black.

The object of the game is to capture the opposing King. When this is done the battle is ended, the side losing whose King is captured. To understand what is meant by the capture of the King it is first necessary to become acquainted with the laws according to which the different men move on the board.

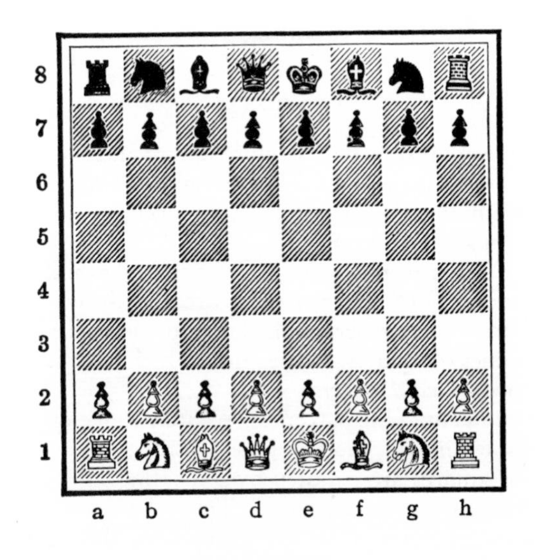

DIAGRAM 1

To start with, the board must be placed so that the players have a white square at their right. Then the men take the positions shown in Diagram 1.

The Rooks occupy the corner squares; next to them stand the Knights; then the Bishops and in the center the King and the Queen.

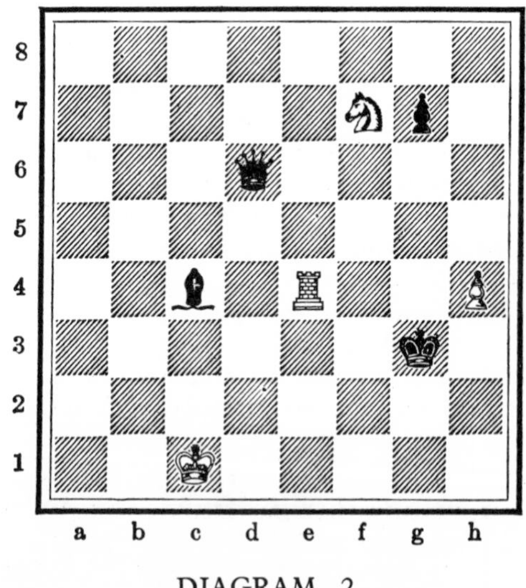

DIAGRAM 2

The white Queen must be on the white square and the black Queen on the black square. These eight men are commonly known as "pieces" in distinction from the Pawns. The latter occupy the line of squares immediately in front of the Pieces.

The lines of squares now occupied by the men and the other four vacant horizontal lines between them are called *ranks*. The vertical lines of squares running perpendicularly to the ranks are called *files*. The oblique lines of squares, that is, lines which connect squares of the same color, are called *diagonals*.

With White starting, the players alternately move one of their men. To describe these moves, the first letters of the names of the pieces are used, and the squares are denoted by indicating the rank and the file of which they form the intersection. This is best accomplished by the so-called algebraic notation which is employed throughout the world except in English, French and Spanish publications where the older rather cumbersome "descriptive notation" has managed to survive. In this book both systems are used. To know both is obviously of advantage to the reader who expects to play tournament Chess, as he will be able to include in his study master games published in Russia and Central Europe, the countries where the strongest Chess is played.

In the algebraic notation the files are lettered from a to h, starting from the file on White's left. The ranks are numbered from 1 to 8, starting from the rank on which White's pieces stand at the beginning of the game. Thus it takes only one letter and one numeral to define clearly the intersection of the rank and the file in which a square is located. The Rook in the position of Diagram 2, for instance, stands on e4, the Bishop on c4, the Pawns on h4 and g7, the Knight on f7, the Queen on d6 and the Kings on c1 and g3.

The English symbol for the Knight is Kt, to distinguish it from K for King, or N (the first letter when spelling Knight phonetically).

In the descriptive notation the symbolization of the squares is more complicated (see page 15).

THE MOVES OF THE MEN

Each of the six kinds of men moves in a different way. To remember the six varieties of moves naturally requires a little more effort than to remember just the one way of moving as in most other board games. But it takes only very little practice to become familiar with the various moves of the Chessman and it is soon revealed to the learner that the variety of the moves enables a surprising depth and wealth of combinations which give keener and greater pleasure to this game than to any other.

The Rook

The Rook may move forward, backward or sideways in a straight line along a path not obstructed by a man of the same color. In other words, he may move to any square of the rank or file on which he stands unless another man of his own color is in the way. If there is a hostile man in the way he may capture him by occupying his square and removing him from the board. In Diagram 2, for instance, the Rook could move to e5, e6, e7, e8, e3, e2, e1, f4, g4, d4, and c4. In making the latter move he would capture the black Bishop. The Rook may not go to h4 because a man of his own color stands there nor may he go to b4 or a4 because he is not allowed to jump over the Bishop. He could, of course, move to either of these squares on his next move after capturing the Bishop.

The Bishop

The Bishop moves along an oblique line, that is, he may move to any square of the diagonals on which he stands unless—as in the case of the Rook—his way is obstructed by a man of his own color. If there is a hostile man in the way he may capture him. In Diagram 2, therefore, the Bishop may move to a2, b3, d5, e6 or, by capturing the Knight, to f7. He may not move, however, to g8, until his next move after capturing the Knight. In the other diagonal all squares, that is, f1, e2, d3, b5 and a6, are accessible to him.

As the Bishop is confined to squares of the same color as the one on which he stood at the beginning of the game he has access only to thirty-two squares of the board, and from this it is evident that the Rook to whom all squares of the board are accessible is a stronger man.

The Queen

The Queen has the power of both Rook and Bishop having the choice of moving to any square of the rank, file or diagonal on which she stands as long as her path is clear. In Diagram 2 the squares to which the Queen may move are, therefore, a3, b4, c5, e7, f8, f4, e5, c7, b8, d1, d2, d3, d4, d5, d7, d8, a6, b6, c6, e6, f6, g6 and h6. Like the Rook and Bishop she has the power of capturing a hostile man by occupying his square.

The Queen is by far the most powerful of the pieces. Later it will be seen that ordinarily her strength is about equal to the strength of two Rooks.

The King

The King, like the Queen, moves and captures in any direction, but he is much less powerful because he may move only one square at a time. Nevertheless, he is the most important man, for, as said at the beginning, the object of each side is the capture of the opposing King.

To save the King from untimely death there is a rule that the King may not move into any square which is in the direct range of any man of his enemy. Thus, in Diagram 2 the black King may move to f2, g2, h2, f3 and h3, but he may not move to f4 or g4 nor may he capture the Pawn on h4, for on any of these squares he could be captured by the white Rook.

The white King in Diagram 2 has only three squares to which he may go, namely, b1, b2 and c2, as the squares d1 and d2, though being in his range, are commanded by the black Queen.

The Knight

The Knight moves neither in rank nor file nor diagonal and, therefore, usually offers a little more difficulty to the beginner than the other pieces. The Knight's move is perhaps best described as a leap to the next but one square of different color.[1] For instance, in Diagram 2 the Knight may move to d8, d6, e5, g5, h6 and h8. In moving to d6 he would capture the Queen.

His move would be in no way obstructed if some of his own or his adversary's men were occupying the squares next to the one on which he stands. This enables the Knight as the only one of the pieces to move at the beginning of the game before any Pawn move has been made.

The strength of the Knight is ordinarily regarded as about equal to that of the Bishop. The latter's range is larger but the Knight has the advantage of being able to reach any square of the board regardless of color.

The Pawn

It remains to describe the move of the Pawn, the only man who captures in a different way from that in which he moves. The Pawn moves *forward only* in the file in which he stands, and only one square at a time with the exception of his first move on which he may advance two squares. Thus, in Diagram 2, the white Pawn may move only to h5 while the black Pawn may move to either g6 or g5.

The Pawn may capture only diagonally, only forward and only one square at a time. The privilege of taking a double step on the first move does not extend to the capture. Thus in Diagram 2, the white Pawn could capture only a black man on g5, the black Pawn only a man on either f6 or h6, but not on e5. If a man stood on h5, the Pawn h4 would be blocked. Likewise would the Pawn on g7 be blocked by a man on g6.

There is one peculiar rule to be remembered in connection with the move of the Pawn. If a Pawn uses his privilege of making a double step

[1] It may be helpful to consider the Knight's move when completed as having described a letter "L" composed of four squares, three in one direction and one at right angles to them.

to avoid capture by a hostile Pawn he can be put back one square and captured just the same. For instance, in Diagram 2, if the white Pawn stood on h5 and Black moved his Pawn to g5, White could put Black's Pawn back to g6 and capture him with his Pawn. This way of capturing is called taking "en passant" (French for "in passing") and can be done only by a Pawn, never by a piece.

Lastly must be mentioned the power of the Pawn to become transformed into a piece. This is done automatically whenever a Pawn reaches the extreme opposite side of the board. That is, the player must remove the Pawn from the board and put any piece on his place except a King. Thus it can happen that a player may play with three or more Rooks, Bishops, Knights or Queens. As the Queen is the strongest piece the Pawns are practically always exchanged for Queens and for this reason the process of the exchange is called "queening."

Although a Pawn has comparatively little value as measured by his mobility—his range of movement—he is really a very valuable man because of the possibility of his eventually queening.

Castling

Only once in a game is a player allowed to move more than one piece at a time. This one move is called "castling" and is made by the King together with one of the Rooks. In castling the King moves two squares

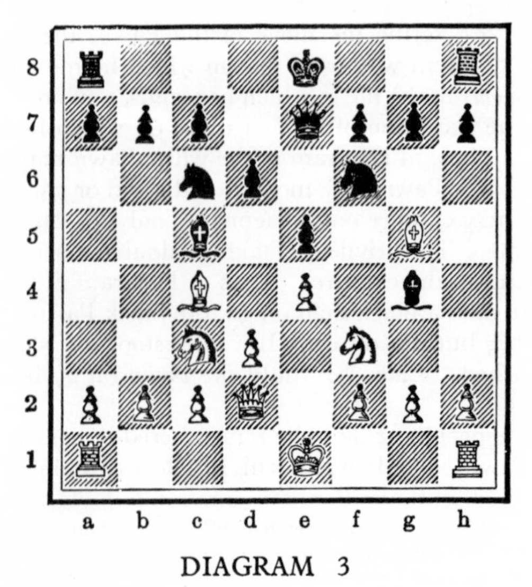

DIAGRAM 3

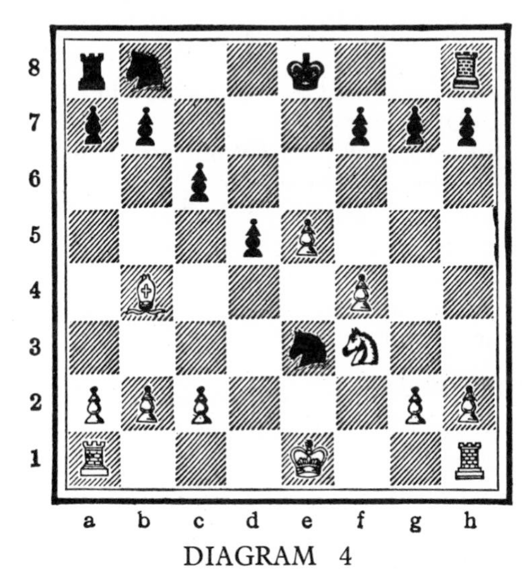

DIAGRAM 4

toward the Rook and the Rook is placed on the square over which the King has passed. In the position of Diagram 3 both players may castle either side.

White, in "castling King's side" would place his King on g1 and the King's Rook on f1; in "castling Queen's side" the King would leap to c1 while the Queen's Rook would take his stand on d1. Likewise Black would castle by either playing the King to g8 and the Rook from h8 to f8, or the King to c8 and the Rook to a8 to d8.

Castling is permitted only when neither King nor Rook concerned has previously moved, when none of the squares between the King and the Rook are obstructed and when none of the three squares involved in the King's move are controlled by an adverse man. Thus if in check (see page 10) the player may not castle. In Diagram 4, neither White nor Black may castle.

SPECIAL TERMS

Attack and Defense

A man is said to *attack* another man if he moves so that on his next move he could capture the other man. Thus, in Diagram 5, White could attack Black's Bishop by moving his Rook to d1 or to e6.

A man is said to *defend* or to *protect* another man if he moves so that in case the other man is captured by a hostile man he could recapture the latter. Thus, in Diagram 5, Black could defend his Bishop by moving his Knight to either e4 or e8 in case White attacks with the Rook from d1. Should White attack from e6, then Black would not defend the Bishop with the Knight, for on e4 as well as on e8 the Knight is unprotected and could be captured by the Rook without White losing anything in exchange. Black has a much more simple way to defend the attack of the Rook from e6, that is, by capturing the Rook with the Pawn f7. For this reason White would not have moved the Rook to e6.

Check and Checkmate

If a man makes a move which attacks the opposing King the King is said to be in "check." The player whose King is checked then has to make a move which gets the King out of check or he forfeits the game.

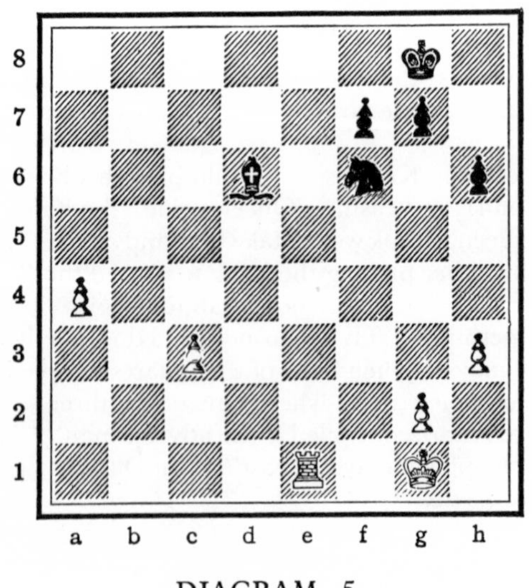

DIAGRAM 5

This is the only case in which a player is not at liberty to make any move he likes.

Unless the attacking man can be captured there are only two ways of getting out of check. One of these is to interpose a man between the King and the attacking piece, and the other to move the King out of the line of attack. In Diagram 5 Black could give check by moving the Bishop to c5. In answer to this White has four moves at his disposal. He may either move the King to f1 or h1 or h2, or he may interpose his Rook on e3. The latter would be very unwise as Black would simply take the Rook with his Bishop, again checking White's King. The situation would then not have changed at all except that White would have lost his Rook. White's King could not move to f2, for this would leave him still attacked by the Bishop.

Instead of checking on c5 Black could have attacked White's King on h2. But in this case the King would have simply captured the Bishop.

If it were White's move he could give check with the Rook on e8. But Black could take the Rook with the Knight. He would naturally do this instead of either moving out with the King to h7 or interposing the Bishop on f8.

If a King is in Check and there is no move with which to get him out

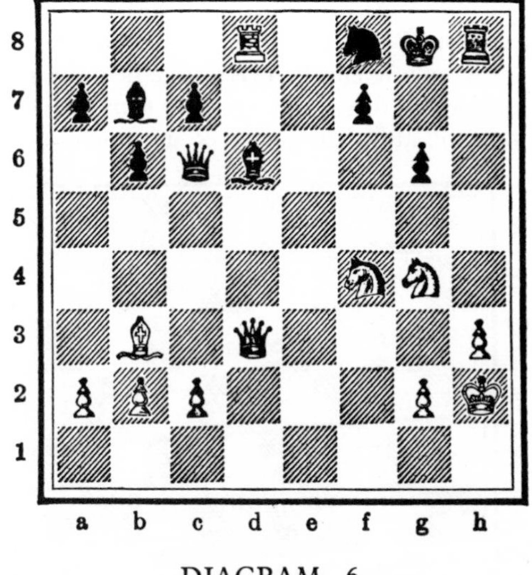

DIAGRAM 6

of it he is said to be "checkmate" and the game is ended. Diagram 6 shows an example in which either player can give checkmate on the move.

If it were White's move he would take the Pawn on g6 with his Queen. Now Black's King is in check as White's Queen threatens to take him on the next move. The King cannot move to either g7 or h7, for these two squares are also commanded by White's Queen. Moreover, the latter cannot be taken by the Pawn on f7 as the black King would be in check by the Bishop on b3. The Pawn is "pinned" by the Bishop. Black's Knight cannot take White's Queen either as he is pinned by White's Rook. Finally, there is no piece available which may be interposed between White's Queen and Black's King; in other words: Black is checkmate, his game is lost.

If it were Black's move he would take the Pawn g2 with the Queen. Now White's King is in check as Black's Queen threatens to take him on the next move. He may not take the Queen as he would then be captured by the Bishop b7. Neither may the Knight f4 take the Queen as he is pinned by the Bishop d6. Moreover, the King may not escape to g1, h1 or g3, these three squares lying in the range of Black's Queen; and so there is no move on the board with which to get White's King out of check: He is checkmate, White loses the game.

Stalemate

If a player, without being in check, cannot make any move which would not get his King into check, he is said to be *stalemate*. In this case the game is considered a draw. Diagram 7 shows an example.

White on the move, although his forces are much inferior, can draw

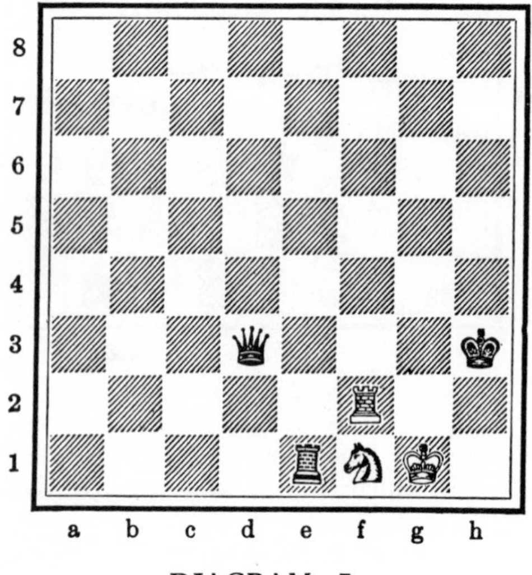

DIAGRAM 7

the game by checking with the Rook on f3. Black cannot very well make a move with his King in reply, as then White's Rook would take the Queen. Black, therefore, must capture the Rook with the Queen and with this move he stalemates White, as the latter has no move left which would not bring his King into check.

If it were Black's move he would easily win. In fact he has two different ways of checkmating White in three moves. One of them

DIAGRAM 8

would be to take the Knight with the Rook, attacking the King and forcing White's Rook to recapture as the King has no square to go to; then to give check with the Queen on g3 forcing White's King to h1 and enabling the mate with the Queen on g2 or h2.

The other way would be to start with the check on g3. As White's Knight is pinned he cannot capture the Queen. Interposing the Rook on g2 would not help either as the Queen would simply take him at the same time checkmating the King. White's only move is, therefore, to play the King into the corner, and Black then mates by first taking the Knight and then moving the Queen to g2 or h2.

Perpetual Check

If a player is able to check the opposing King continually and he indicates his intention to do so the game is considered a draw. In the diagramed position, for instance, White on the move can draw the game by giving a perpetual check on e8 and h5. Black cannot help himself as he has to go back and forth with the King on h7 and g8. Without the possibility of this perpetual check White would be lost, for he cannot prevent the Pawn a2 from queening and with two Queens against one Black would easily win as will be seen later from the discussion of elementary endings.

Exchange

To exchange means to capture a hostile man when it allows a man of the same value to be captured by the opponent.

It is rather confusing that the term "exchange" is also used for the difference in value between a Rook and a Bishop or a Knight. To win the exchange, in this sense, means to capture a Rook and to lose for it only a Bishop or a Knight.

Double Pawn

Two pawns of the same player standing in one file are called a double Pawn. Three Pawns in one file are called a triple Pawn.

Passed Pawn

A Pawn whose advance to the eighth rank is not blocked by an opposing Pawn in the same file and who does not have to pass one on an adjoining file is called a passed Pawn.

Isolated Pawn

A Pawn is called isolated if there are no Pawns of the same player on the adjoining files.

Backward Pawn

A Pawn is called backward if he cannot advance far enough to be protected by fellow Pawns in an adjoining file.

Fork

A Pawn is said to fork two pieces if he attacks them simultaneously.

Minor Piece

The Bishops and the Knights are called minor Pieces as compared with the Rooks and the Queen.

Sacrifice

To sacrifice means to give up a man without obtaining for him a man of the opponent or to give up a man for one of lesser value.

Discovered Check and Double Check

A discovered Check is an attack on the King caused by a man moving out of the line of a piece which he was obstructing. If the man discovering the Check also attacks the King the Check is called a double Check.

SYMBOLS FOR MOVES

Algebraic Notation

In addition to the symbols used for squares and men, as explained on page 5, the following are used to indicate the moves:

– means "moves to"

× means "captures"

o–o means "Castles King's side"

o–o–o means "Castles Queen's side"

+ means "check"

± means "checkmate"

Thus: R–f5 means the Rook moves to square f5. If either Rook could move to f5 then the original square of the Rook to be moved must also be shown.

Kte3×d5 means the Knight standing on e3 captures the man standing on d5.

o–o–o + means the player castles Queen's side and in so doing gives check.

! signifies a good move.

? signifies a bad move.

Descriptive Notation

In the descriptive notation alluded to on page 5 every square of the board has two different names, each player counting the ranks from his own side. The files are named after the pieces which stand on them at the beginning of the game. Thus, c4 would be QB4 (Queen's Bishop's fourth) or QB5 depending on whether a black or a white move is described. If a square is referred to without relation to a particular move it is necessary to add from which side of the board the square is counted. It is customary to say in cases of this kind "White's Queen's fourth" or "Black's Queen's fourth," etc.

Instead of naming the square on which a capture takes place, the man captured is named, so that an additional description is necessary in case more than one man of the same kind can be captured.

As a matter of comparison the first ten moves of a game are described below in both notations.

(1)	P-d4	P-d5	(1)	P-Q4	P-Q4
(2)	P-c4	P-e6	(2)	P-QB4	P-K3
(3)	Kt-c3	P-c5	(3)	Kt-QB3	P-QB4
(4)	Kt-f3	Kt-c6	(4)	Kt-B3	Kt-QB3
(5)	Pxd5	Pxd5	(5)	PxQP	KPxP
(6)	B-f4	Kt-f6	(6)	B-KB4	Kt-B3
(7)	P-e3	B-e6	(7)	P-K3	B-K3
(8)	B-d3	B-e7	(8)	B-Q3	B-K7
(9)	o-o	o-o	(9)	Castles	Castles
(10)	R-c1	Kt-h5	(10)	R-B1	Kt-KR4

CHESS LAWS

If a player having the move touches one of his men he is compelled to move him; if he touches a hostile man he must capture him. This law is void, however, if the man so touched cannot be legally moved or captured.

A man may be moved to any square accessible to him as long as the hand of the player has not left him. If an illegal move has been made it must be retracted and if possible another move must be made with the same man. If a player has castled illegally, King and Rook must be moved back and the King must make another move, if there is a legal one.

If a player touches a man with the sole object of adjusting his position, he must indicate his intention by saying "j'adoube" (French for: I adjust) beforehand. In castling, the King must be moved first as otherwise a doubt might arise whether castling or a Rook's move only was intended.

A game is void if a mistake has been made in setting up board or men

(1) Q-f5, K-c6; (2) Q-e5, K-d7; (3) K-c4, K-c6; (4) Q-e7, K-b6; (5) Q-d7, K-a6. White must now be very careful to avoid a stalemate which would result if he deprived the King of all mobility without attacking him at the same time. This would be the case if he now moved Q-c7. For then Black could not move the King to b5, as this square is controlled by White's King, and he could not go to any of the other four squares in his range on account of White's Queen attacking all of them. The correct move is (6) K-c5. This leaves only the square a5 for Black's King, and White checkmates by (7) Q-a7 or (7) Q-b5.

If, in Diagram 9, White had a Rook on h3 instead of the Queen, the mating process would take a few more moves, but there would be no escape for Black either.

It will again be White's aim to confine Black's King to a smaller and smaller number of squares. The best way to start will therefore be (1) R-e3. No matter what Black replies, he cannot prevent White from driving him to the edge of the board in a similar way to the one shown in the following example:

(1) . . ., K-d5; (2) R-e1. This is a *waiting move*. Black must leave d5, thus enabling either White's King to advance or the Rook to occupy e5. (2) . . ., K-c5; (3) R-e5; K-d6; (4) K-d4, K-c6; (5) R-d5, K-b6; (6) R-c5, K-b7; (7) K-d5, K-b6; (8) K-d6, K-b7; (9) R-b5, K-a6; (10) K-c6, K-a7; (11) K-c7, K-a6; (12) R-h5, K-a7; (13) R-a5 mate.

The two examples discussed show that it is not necessary to drive th King into the corner but that he can be mated on any square of th edge by Queen or Rook. It will be observed that in the mating positio three of the six squares at Black's disposal are controlled by White King and the other three by the Rook (or the Queen). If White ha only a Bishop or a Knight in addition to the King he could never ma Black, for neither Bishop nor Knight can attack the King and at t same time control a square adjacent to the King. This, however, is least necessary to force the mate, even in the most unfavora position of the King, that is, in the corner.

There are possibilities of a player mating his opponent with King and Knight or King and Bishop, but then there must be a ma the opponent blocking the escape of the King. Diagram 10 is an ample of such a case. White plays (1) Kt-c5, K-h1; (2) Kt-e4. Black cannot continue with P-h2, as White would checkmate Kt-g3. Therefore, he must play (2) . . ., K-h2. White then ge Knight in such a position as to deprive Black's King of the escape and to keep the square g3 accessible to the Knight: (3) Kt-d2

or if in the course of the game the position or number of men have been altered in a manner not in accordance with the rules of play and the position cannot be reconstructed from the point where the error was made.

If a player resigns his game before he is actually mated he acknowledges that in the end mate is unavoidable, and the game is counted as a loss to him.

If neither player has sufficient material left to enforce a mate (compare following chapter) the game is considered a draw. A draw may also be claimed by either player if fifty moves have been made without the capture of a man or the move of a Pawn, except in the rare cases in which it can be proved that more than fifty moves are required to force a mate.

When a position has recurred in a game three times with the same player on the move, either player may claim a draw. It is immaterial whether or not the order of the moves which led to a repetition of the position has been the same every time, or whether during those moves either King's Rook and Queen's Rook or King's Knight and Queen's Knight have exchanged places.

II

ELEMENTARY TACTICS

The beginner who thinks he ought to be able to play a good game of Chess after learning the moves of the men is like the soldier who is confident that he could lead an army after he has learned how to march.

He may have great strategical gifts but he will not be able to use them to any advantage unless he is thoroughly conversant with the tactical possibilities afforded by the coöperation of the different units of which his army is composed and by the topography of the ground on which the battle takes place.

The different conditions of the battle ground in war which make some positions more easily accessible to infantry than to artillery and vice versa have their equivalent on the Chess board in the different ways in which the men move and which make certain squares accessible to some of them which others cannot reach.

The first thing, then, for the beginner to do is to acquaint himself thoroughly with the characteristic features of each man so that he may know exactly how much work to expect from him. The best way to accomplish this is the study of the elementary problems which are in end games, that is, in positions where only a few men are left on each side.

FUNDAMENTAL ENDINGS

Considering that the object of the game is the capture of the opposing King, it seems most important to find out whether there are positions in which this capture can be accomplished in the face of the best possible defense. Naturally a player must have a certain material superiority to be able to force a mate, and the first question which offers itself is what *minimum* force is required to compel the surrender of a King whose men have all been captured during the game.

It is clear that in order to checkmate the lone King it is necessary to attack the square on which he stands as well as all adjacent squares to which he could escape. The most unfavorable position for the King is,

of course, a corner of the board as there he has only three square to while in the middle of the board eight squares are accessible to Consequently, in an ending in which one player has only his King the other player will try to drive the King into a corner where he n control over only three additional squares.

It can easily be seen that this can be done without difficulty wi King and Queen or with King and Rook. Supposing, for instanc White has his King on c3 and his Queen on h3 while Black's King stands on d6 as shown in the following diagram.

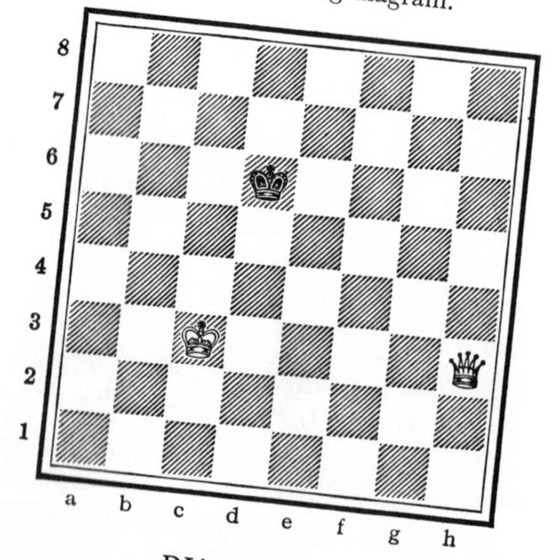

DIAGRAM 9

How will White proceed in order to drive the King into a corner and checkmate him there?

A direct onslaught with the Queen on e6 or d7 is clearly not advisable as the Queen would not be protected on these squares, so that the King could simply capture her. A long range attack from h2, g3, d3 or h6 is not effective either as it would not restrict the mobility of the King who could go to either d5 or e6 or e5, that is away from the corner to which he is to be driven.

The correct way of maneuvering for White will be to confine Black's King to a smaller and smaller territory until he finally has to back up against the side or the corner of the board. This consideration indicates the following line of play:

Kt-g3, which would stalemate Black's King), K-h1; (4) Kt-f1. The only move left to Black is now P-h2, and White mates by (5) Kt-g3.

If it were Black's move in the position of the Diagram the game would be a draw, for after (1) . . ., K-h1; (2) Kt-c5, P-h2 Black is stalemate unless White moves his King so as to make the square g1 accessible

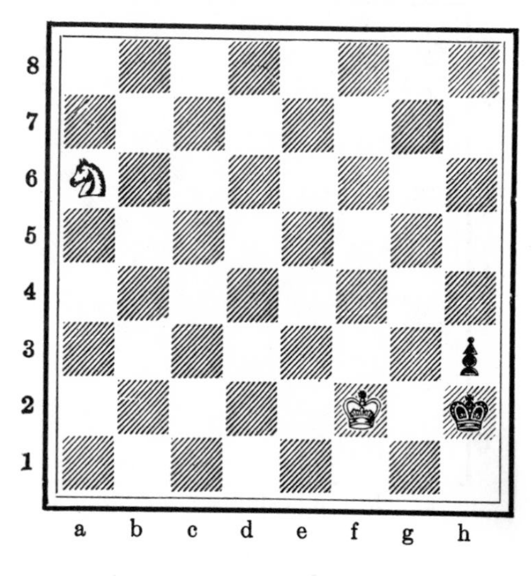

DIAGRAM 10

to Black. However, he will not do that as it would enable Black to queen the Pawn and to win the game.

In the case of King and Bishop against King and another man a mate can only occur through a blunder. Supposing for instance White has the King on f3 and a Bishop on d5 and Black has the King on h1 and a Bishop or a Pawn on h2, then White on the move would mate by K-f2. But it is evident that Black must have made a blunder, for on the move preceding the position of the Diagram he must have either played his King into the corner or moved the Bishop or Pawn to h2, both moves which were in no way forced.

To checkmate with King and two Bishops against King or with Bishop and Knight against King offers no difficulty. The only thing the player must keep in mind is that he needs his King for the drive. The two pieces are not sufficient to confine the opposing King to the corner. In Diagram 11 for instance, it will be the best policy for White to advance right away with his King in order to prevent Black's King from escaping into the middle of the board. The following play might then ensue:

(1) K-b2, K-b7; (2) K-c3, K-c6; (3) K-d4, K-d6; (4) B-f5, K-c6; (5) B-f4, K-b5; (6) B-e4, K-b4; (7) B-d3, K-b3; (8) B-d2, K-b2; (9) K-c4, K-a3; (10) K-c3, K-a4; (11) K-c2 (not K-b2 which would stalemate

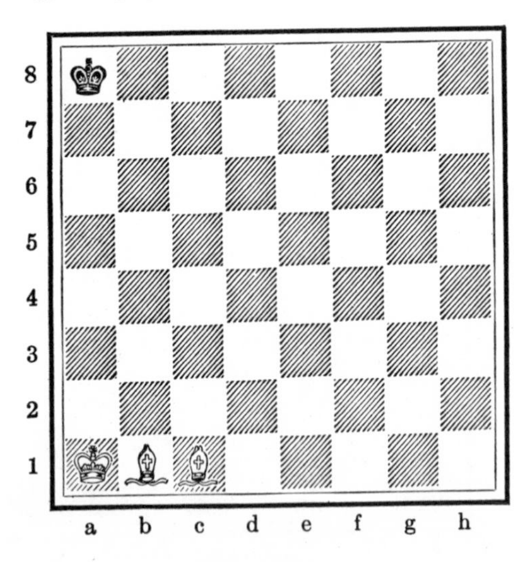

DIAGRAM 11

Black's King), K-a3; (12) B-b5, K-a2; (13) B-c1, K-a1; (14) B-b2, K-a2; (15) B-c4 mate.

In the fight of King, Bishop and Knight against the King the mate can be enforced only in a corner controlled by the Bishop, if the lone King always makes the best move. Diagram 12 may serve as an example of this ending. White has a black Bishop and so he will have to drive Black's King to either h8 or a1 as it is not possible to mate him in the white corner a8, unless he makes a blunder.

After (1) B-e5 for instance, Black must of course not go into the corner as Kt-b6 would mate him. He will play K-c8 and White will have to prevent the flight of the black King into the middle of the board. It is easy to see, by the way, that the Kt cannot be placed so as to control the square c8, thereby forcing the King into the corner, and to threaten the mate on b6 at the same time. For he can control c8 only from a black square while he would have to stand on a white square to be able to reach b6 in one move.

After (1) B-e5, K-c8; (2) K-b6, K-d7; (3) Kt-f4 Black's King is confined to the seventh and eighth ranks and it is only a question of time when he will be forced to h8: White's Bishop being only capable of commanding black squares the Knight will have to be used to drive the King from white squares. For instance: K-c8; (4) K-c6, K-d8; (5)

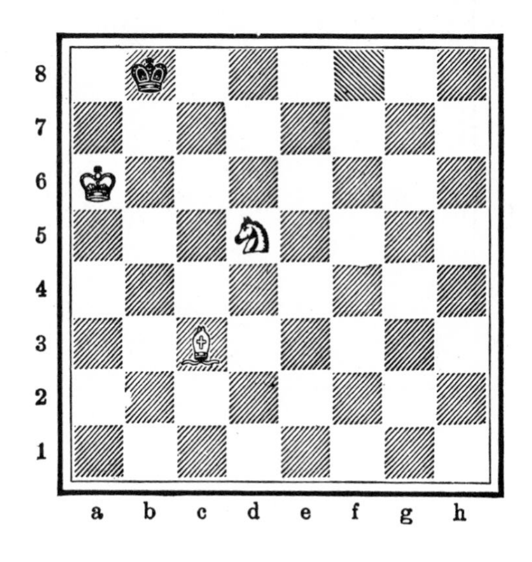

DIAGRAM 12

Kt-g6, K-c8; (6) Kt-e7, K-d8; (7) K-d6, K-e8; (8) K-e6, K-d8; (9) B-h2. A waiting move. White wants to place the Bishop on c7 so as to make d8 inaccessible to Black. (9) K-e8; (10) B-c7, K-f8; (11) Kt-f5, K-e8; (12) Kt-g7, K-f8; (13) K-f6, K-g8; (14) K-g6, K-f8; (15) B-d6, K-g8; (16) Kt-f5, K-h8; (17) B-a3. Again a waiting move. White cannot play Kt-h6 right away as Black would be stalemate. (17) . . ., K-g8; (18) Kt-h6, K-h8; (19) B-b2 mate.

It is not possible to force a mate with King and two Knights, for even if a position similar to Diagram 13 is arrived at, in which the King can be driven into the corner, the Knight who prevents the King from escaping is never ready to give the checkmate, and in order to prevent a stalemate the other Knight would have to let the King out of the corner again. If Black had a spare move, for instance if he had a Pawn left, then White would win. (1) Kt-a6, K-a8; (2) Kt-e8, Pawn moves; (3) Kt-c7 mate.

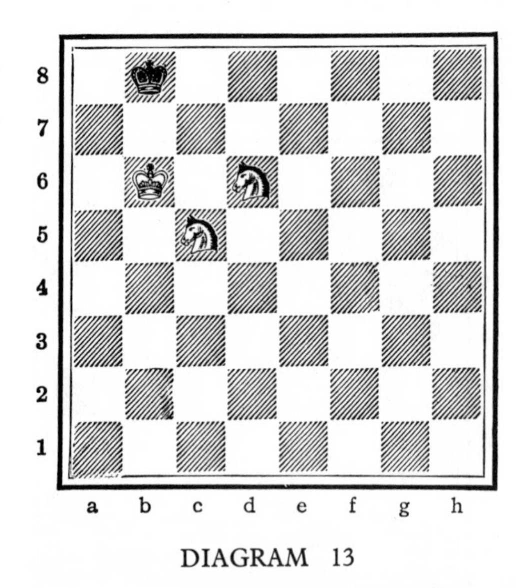

DIAGRAM 13

RELATIVE VALUE OF THE MEN

From the foregoing examples it is possible to form a vague idea of the strength of the different pieces. The Queen is apparently the strongest piece. On account of her superior mobility she can confine the hostile King with a few moves and force him into a mating net. Of the other pieces the Rook is no doubt the strongest for he is sufficient to force a mate in conjunction with his own King, while Bishop or Knight cannot do so. Two Bishops apparently are stronger than two Knights, while it is not possible yet to say anything about the relative value of one Bishop and one Knight.

The above valuation, however, holds good only on the comparatively vacant board, where the pieces can make full use of their mobility. It is the mobility alone which decides the value of a man, and positions often occur in which a Knight is more valuable than a Rook or in which a Pawn might be preferable to a Bishop and so on. The reason is that sometimes the weaker man occupies a commanding square while the stronger man is obstructed somehow or other so that he cannot be made to work. Examples for positions of this kind will be discussed in the Chapter on combination.

Although it is impossible to indicate exactly the relative value of the men in each position, experience enables a fair estimation of their average strength. The Queen is about as strong as two Rooks or as three minor pieces (Bishops or Knights). A minor piece is about equivalent to three Pawns, and a Rook is consequently equal to a minor piece and one to two Pawns.

The value of a Pawn is the hardest thing to grasp for the beginner. A Pawn appears to be of so little use on account of his limited mobility, that it seems hardly worth while to waste time on saving a Pawn that is attacked, as so much greater things are apparently at issue. What he overlooks is the latent value of the Pawn which lies in the possibility of queening him later in the game.

To realize the importance of the Pawn it is necessary to know exactly under what conditions he *can* be queened. This knowledge is all the more indispensable to the Chess player as the vast majority of all games finally resolve themselves into Pawn endings in which the advantage of one or more Pawns decides the issue.

In most of these cases some pieces are on the board in addition to the Pawns and sometimes it is only by their exchange that the game can be won. The most elementary example is that shown in Diagram 14.

White is a Pawn ahead and it will be his object to Queen it. The beginner, in his haste to advance the Pawn, will probably play P-e5 at once and lose the Pawn, as Black can answer Q-d4 check with simultaneous attack on the Pawn. The correct way to play for White is (1) Q-d1+, K-a3 or b4; (2) Qxa4, Kxa4. Now that the Queens are exchanged White need not any longer worry about any interference with his plans to queen the Pawn except maneuvers of the black King, which might still lead to the capture or the blockade of the Pawn.

A rash advance of the Pawn would again be the wrong thing. The right way of playing is indicated by a simple calculation. The Pawn needs four moves to reach the queening square. But the black King arrives there in the same number of moves, so that he can capture the Pawn the moment he queens. Consequently White will only be able to enforce the safe queening of his Pawn if he can gain control of the queening square with his own King, thus protecting the Pawn at the time of queening.

Now, White needs three moves to bring his King up to his Pawn on f4. In the meantime Black will have reached the square d6 and after White's (4) K-f5 Black will block the further advance of White's King by K-e7. However, White can force Black to give the way free. The maneuver by which he does this is one which occurs in a similar form in nearly all Pawn endings and its thorough grasp is therefore essential. Diagram 15 shows the critical position.

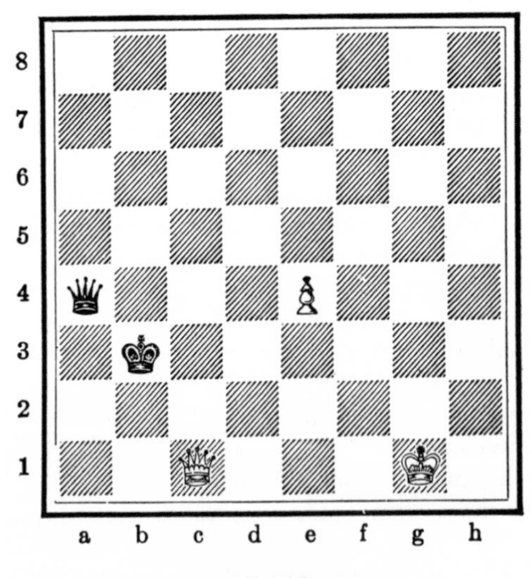

DIAGRAM 14

White can win the game only by playing (5) K-e5. The technical term for this move is "going into *Opposition.*" The Kings oppose each other in one line on squares of the same color and the one who has to move out of opposition—in this case Black's King—is compelled to allow the advance of the opposing King to the next line. If Black plays K-d7, White answers (6) K-f6, and if Black plays K-f7, (6) K-d6 would follow. Then, after Black's K-e8, White repeats the maneuver by taking the opposition with (7) K-e6, and again Black must back out with either K-d8 or K-f8, so that White can advance to either f7 or d7. This clears the way for the Pawn who now advances unimpeded to the queening square.

The important rôle which the opposition of the Kings play in Pawn endings is still more strikingly illustrated by the situations which would result if in the position of Diagram 15 White played (5) P-e5 instead of K-e5. Black would then draw the game by maintaining the opposition himself. He would play K-f7 and although after (6) P-e6, K-e7; (7) K-e5 White has regained the opposition he cannot keep it if Black continues correctly. The move which saves the game for Black is K-e8. K-d8 or K-f8 lose, as then White could go into opposition by K-d6 or K-f6. The play in these three cases would be this: A: (7) . . ., K-e8, (8) K-f6, K-f8; (9) P-e7+, K-e8; (10) K-e6 and Black is stale-

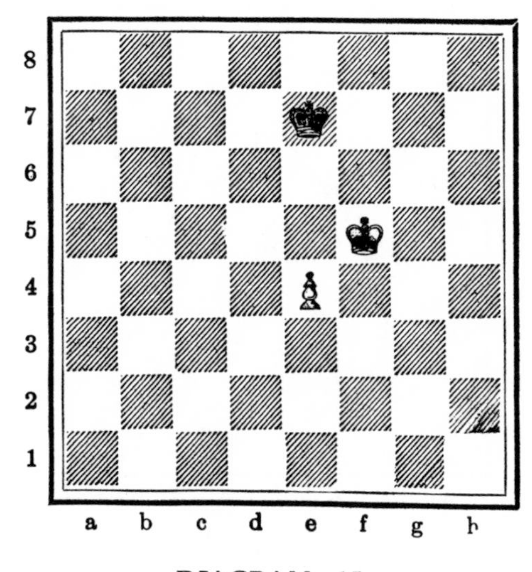

DIAGRAM 15

mate, the game is drawn. B: (7) . . ., K-d8; (8) K-d6, K-e8; (9) P-e7 and Black must move K-f7 enabling White to obtain control of the queening square by (10) K-d7. C: (7) . . ., K-f8, (8) K-f6, K-e8, etc., similar to the play in B.

To sum up the investigation of this Pawn ending: The deciding factor is the opposition of the Kings on the 6th and 8th ranks. If the weaker party succeeds in obtaining that opposition with the Pawn on the 6th rank he draws the game.

If the Pawn is not yet advanced to the 6th rank the opposition of the Kings is of no avail to the weaker party as the Pawn advancing would force the opposing King out of opposition again. Suppose, for instance, White has the King on e6 and the Pawn on e5 while Black's King stands on e8 with White on the move. White must get out of opposition by playing K-f6 or K-d6 and Black keeps the opposition by K-f8 or K-d8. But then White has a move to spare which forces Black out of opposition and thereby wins the game. He plays P-e6 and the game ends in the way discussed above.

The ending King and Pawn against King is one of the most important for every Chess player to know, not only because a great number of positions can be reduced to this ending by the exchange of all the other

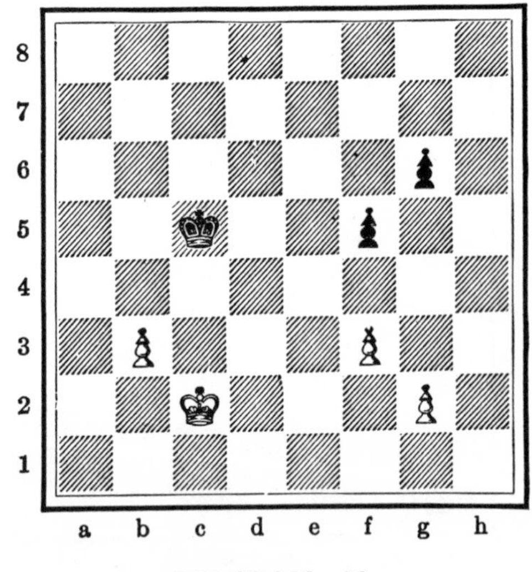

DIAGRAM 16

men left on the board, but also because it gives the first insight into the peculiar maneuvers of the King which have to be carried out in connection with gaining or giving up the opposition, and which, as will be seen later on, constitute the essence of the most frequent pawn endings.

For the beginner, of course, the opposition maneuvers are rather difficult to grasp and it is fortunate for him that the vast majority of pawn endings are of a much simpler form. The winning maneuver in these endings into which most Chess games resolve themselves, is easily explained and after understanding it the beginner can readily see the fundamental principle underlying every game.

Diagram 16 shows a typical position on which the winning method should be studied. White is a pawn ahead, but as demonstrated on the position of Diagram 15 he cannot queen his passed Pawn because his King is not in front of it. On the other hand, there cannot possibly be any advantage in advancing the Pawns on the other side of the board as there Black has the same number of Pawns as White and consequently there is no reason why one of the white Pawns should succeed in breaking through. It is all the same very easy for White to win and the strategy to be employed will be evident from the following consideration: Black's King is considerably confined in his movements as he has to be constantly watching White's passed Pawn. White's King,

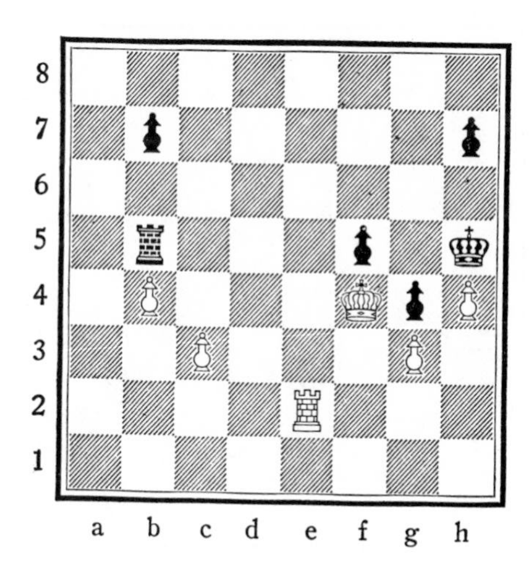

DIAGRAM 17

however, is free to go wherever he likes without any immediate danger. There is consequently nothing to hinder him attacking and capturing the black Pawns, for if Black's King tries to stop White's advance, White's passed Pawn marches on and compels the opposing King to catch him, thereby giving the way free to his own King. According to this scheme play could proceed like this: (1) K-d3, K-d5; (2) K-e3, K-e5; (3) P-b4, P-g5; (4) P-b5, K-d5; (5) P-b6, K-c6; (6) K-d4, Kxb6; (7) K-e5, P-f4; (8) K-f5, K-c6; (9) Kxg5, K-d6; (10) Kxf4, K-e6; (11) K-g5, K-f7. Now White would win even without the Pawn g2 by playing (12) K-f5 and so on as explained in Diagram 15.

From the foregoing it will be clear to the beginner that if a player succeeds in winning a Pawn he can win the game if he is able to exchange all pieces so that only the Pawns are left. However, he will not yet see the way in which this exchange of pieces can be forced. It is evident that the player who has lost the Pawn will try to avoid the exchange, hoping that he may be able to regain the Pawn with his pieces. Therefore, he will permit his opponent an exchange only if, in avoiding it, he would sustain an additional loss. The position of Diagram 17 offers a simple example. White on the move will play R-e5, offering the exchange of Rooks. If Black tried to avoid the exchange by playing R-b6, White would capture the Pawn f5 with the

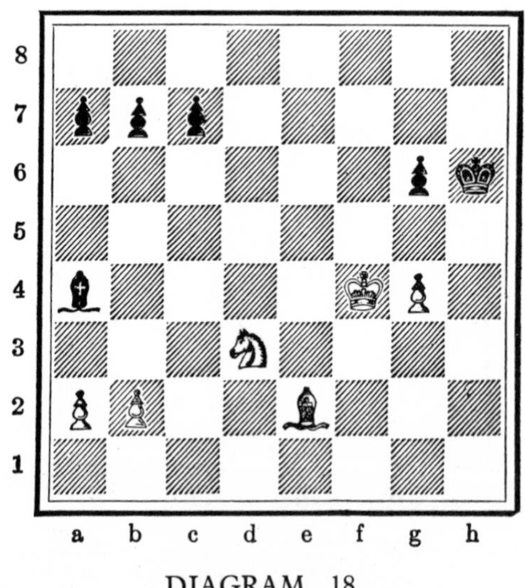

DIAGRAM 18

Rook and after Black's King moves out of check he would take the Pawn g4 too. Therefore Black has to make the offered exchange of Rooks, and White then wins by advancing the c-Pawn which forces Black's King over to the Queen's wing and leaves the Pawns of the King's wing unprotected.

The beginner might think that inasmuch as the loss of a Pawn in most cases means the loss of the game on account of the final promotion of the Pawn to the Queen, it may be advisable to sacrifice a piece if thereby the loss of a Pawn can be avoided. However, this idea, which is frequently met, is altogether wrong as the additional piece will easily enable the opponent to gain as many Pawns as he likes within the further course of the game. The position of Diagram 18 may serve as an example. In the following line of play it is assumed that Black makes the best moves, but the method employed is the same for any defensive maneuvers which Black might try, with the only difference that White would win still more quickly. (1) Kt-c5, B-c6; (2) B-f3, Bxf3; (3)

Kxf3, P-b6; (4) Kt-e6, P-c5; (5) P-a4. This move retains the black Pawns so that the Knight can attack them with better effect. (5) . . ., P-c4; (6) Kt-c7, K-g7; (7) Kt-b5, P-a6; (8) Kt-d6, Kt-f6; (9) Ktxc4, P-b5; (10) Pxb5, Pxb5; (11) Kt-a3, P-b4; (12) Kt-c2, P-b3; (13) Kt-d4, etc.

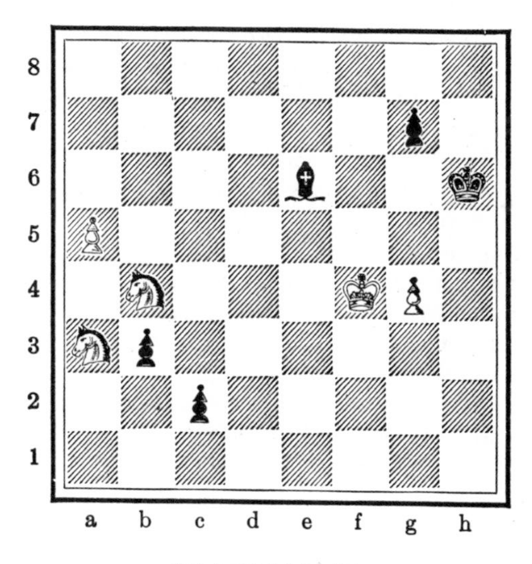

DIAGRAM 19

Often it happens that a player can give up his additional piece to advantage for one or two Pawns thereby enforcing an ending which is won on account of the Pawn position. Diagram 19 is an example.

Black is a piece down but his two connected passed Pawns constitute a dangerous threat. White, therefore, does best to sacrifice a Knight for the two Pawns, as he then remains with two Pawns against one. Black must finally give up his Bishop for White's a-Pawn who threatens to queen, and then White wins by capturing Black's g-Pawn and queening his own. Play might proceed as follows: (1) Ktxc2, Pxc2; (2) Ktxc2, B-d5; (3) Kt-b4, B-a8; (4) P-a6, K-g6; (5) P-a7, K-f6; (6) Kt-a6, K-e7; (7) Kt-c7, B-h1; (8) P-a8 (Queen), Bxa8; (9) Ktxa8, K-f6; (10) Kt-c7, K-g6; (11) Kt-d5, K-h6; (12) K-f5, K-h7; (13) K-g5, K-h8; (14) K-g6, K-g8; (15) Kt-e7+, K-h8; (16) Kt-f5, K-g8; (17) Ktxg7, K-h8; (18) K-f7, K-h7; (19) P-g5, K-h8; (20) Kt-f5, White could not play P-g6, as Black would have been stalemate. (20) . . ., K-h7; (21) P-g6+, K-h8; (22) P-g7+, K-h7; (23) P-g8 (Queen) mate.

The game endings discussed up to now have illustrated the method of winning with a superior force and it is now possible for the beginner to understand that the leading rule for all maneuvers is to *avoid the loss of material*—no matter how small—as it will ultimately lead to the loss of the game by one pawn or the other queening.

The next step will be to find out under what conditions it is possible to gain a man and when it will be possible to avoid loss. To understand the attacking and defensive maneuvers involved it is necessary first to become acquainted with the different ways in which the various pieces can be made to do some useful work, where their strength lies and where their weakness, and how they are able to coöperate. Not before all this is clear to the beginner—in the outlines at least—will he be in a position to play a sensible game or even to understand the most elementary strategic principles.

The reader is therefore urged to study carefully the next chapter in which the characteristic features of the different men are discussed. In this way he will much more quickly arrive at a fair playing strength than by relying on the experience which he may gain in playing a great number of games, trying to find out everything for himself instead of profiting by the knowledge which has been gathered by others in centuries of study.

HOW THE DIFFERENT MEN COÖPERATE

There are two kinds of elementary attack. One when a single man attacks two or more hostile men at the same time; the other when more men are brought up to attack an opposing man than can be mustered for defense. The beginner, as a rule, makes attacks with the sole aim of driving away a hostile piece; it is clear that these attempts will in most cases be futile as they generally allow the attacked piece to move to another square just as or perhaps more favourable. The advantage of attacking two men at once is evident in that probably only one of them can be saved. The advantage of bringing up more men for attack than can be gathered for defense is not less obvious, but will be found more difficult to carry out. Using both methods of attack in conjunction is the secret of the successful coöperation of the men.

In the following diagrams simple illustrations are shown of elementary cases of such attacks. These positions often occur in games of beginners on account of their placing the men on unfavorable squares. In studying them the eye of the beginner will become accustomed to dangerous formations of the pieces and he will be able to foresee similar threats in his games. This is especially true of the mating positions which are discussed below in connection with attacks insti-

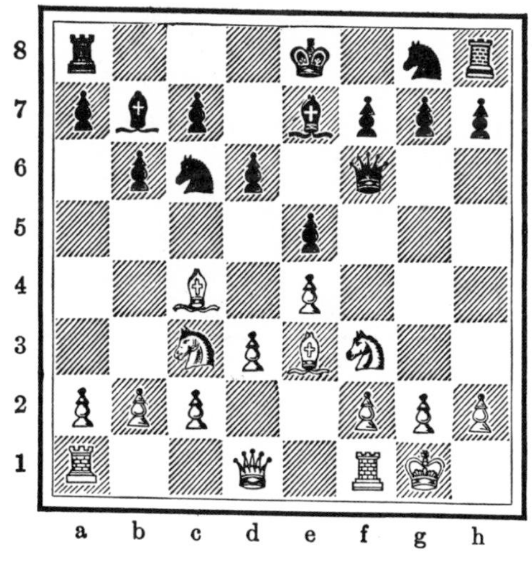

DIAGRAM 20

tuted by the Queen in the middle of the game. It is these attacks to which the beginner at an early stage of the game falls victim in ninety out of a hundred cases when playing against an experienced opponent.

In the position of Diagram 20 White on the move wins the exchange and thereby practically the game by playing (1) Kt-d5. With this move he attacks the Queen and at the same time the Pawn c7. Black, in order not to lose the Queen, must move her, but he cannot move her so that she will protect the Pawn c7. On the next move White will, therefore, take the Pawn calling Check and at the same time attacking the Rook a8. The King must move and the Knight takes the Rook.

Quite frequently a similar attack with the Knight is likely to win the Queen if the opponent is not familiar with situations of that kind. If in the position of Diagram 21 White plays (1) Kt-d5, Black must protect the Pawn c7 by Q-d8 or Q-d6, but not by Q-c6; for in the latter case White would continue with (2) B-b5, Qxb5; (3) Ktxc7+ and (4) Ktxb5.

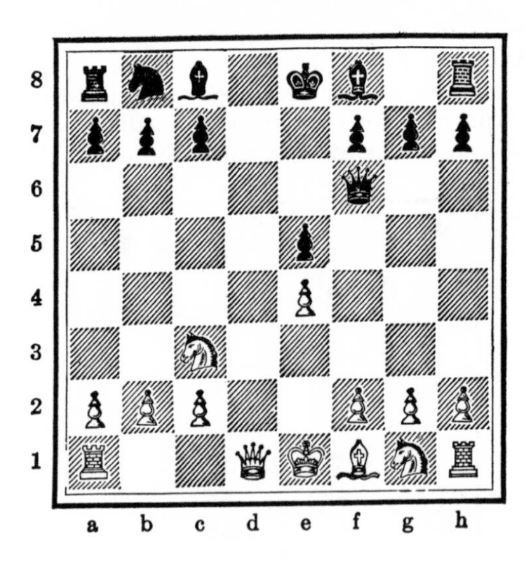

DIAGRAM 21

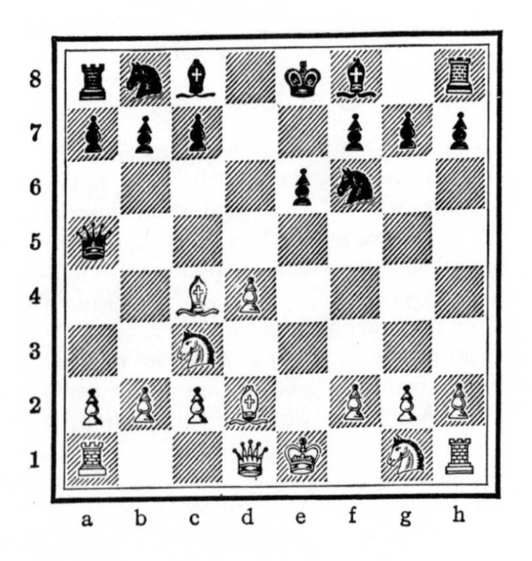

DIAGRAM 22

Sometimes two pieces are involved in the double attack, the line of one of the pieces being discovered by the other. Thus, in the position of Diagram 22, which could be brought about by the moves (1) P-e4, P-d5; (2) Pxd5, Qxd5; (3) Kt-c3, Q-a5; (4) P-d4, Kt-f6; (5) B-c4, P-e6; (6) B-d2, white threatens to play (7) Kt-d5, uncovering the Bishop

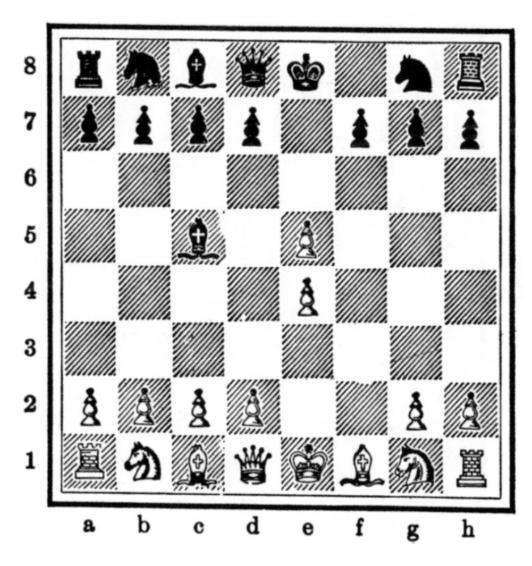

DIAGRAM 23

d2 on Black's Queen and at the same time attacking the Pawn c7, which Black cannot keep protected.

Threats of this kind more frequently occur in connection with a discovered Check. As an example the following opening will serve: (1) P-e4, P-e5; (2) Kt-f3, Kt-f6; (3) Ktxe5, Ktxe4; (4) Q-e2, Kt-f6. Black's last move exposes his King to a discovered Check, and White wins the Queen by playing (5) Kt-c6+.

Next to the Knight the Queen is most frequently in a position to carry out a double attack. Two typical examples are shown in the following diagrams.

After the opening moves (1) P-e4, P-e5; (2) P-f4, B-c5; (3) Pxe5?? the position of Diagram 23 is reached, in which Black wins a Rook by Q-h4+. White cannot reply (4) K-e2 on account of Qxe4 mate. His only move is (4) P-g3 and then follows Qxe4 attacking King and Rook simultaneously.

This opening offers another opportunity to demonstrate the dangerous mobility of the Queen. Instead of (3) Pxe5 White should have played (3) Kt-f3. The game could then have continued as follows: P-d6; (4) B-c4, Kt-f6; (5) Pxe5, Pxe5. Again White cannot win the Pawn e5 for (6) Ktxe5 would be answered by Q-d4, attacking Knight and Bishop and threatening mate on f2.

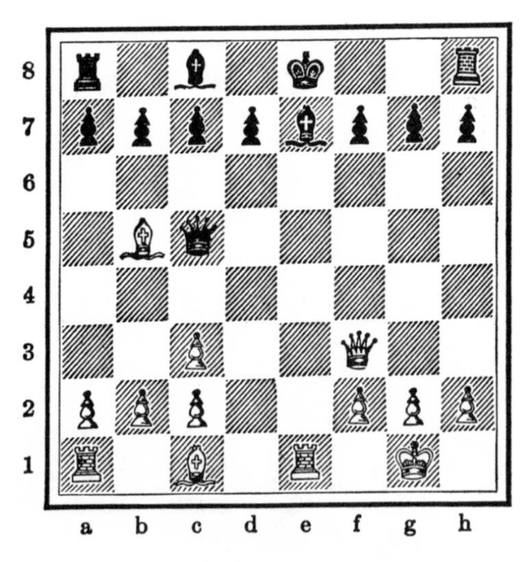

DIAGRAM 24

Diagram 24 shows a typical case of a double threat with the Queen in conjunction with other pieces. White on the move plays B-d3, and now Black cannot castle as White would continue with Q-e4 threatening mate through Qxh7 and at the same time attacking the Bishop e7 for the second time who is only once protected. Black would have to defend the mate by either P-g6 or P-f5 or Q-h5 and White would capture the Bishop.

When castling on the King side a player must always beware of an attack by the Queen and another piece on the King's Rook's Pawn. In the case illustrated above it was the Bishop who assisted the Queen. A Knight could aid in an attack on h7 from either g5 or f6. More frequently he does so from g5 as usually the square f6 is not accessible to him on account of the Pawn g7 protecting it. In the majority of cases the Knight goes to g5 from f3, and the Queen attacks h7 from h5, coming from her original square d1. Then, if Black cannot protect h7 by a Knight from f6 or by the Bishop, from f5 for instance, or from g6, the only protection as a rule is to advance the Pawn to h6. The position of Diagram 25 may serve as an example.

Black's last move was Kt-e7, while Kt-f6, which protects the Pawn h7 against future attacks, is generally preferable in any opening. White can now play Kt-g5, attacking the Pawn f7 for the second time,

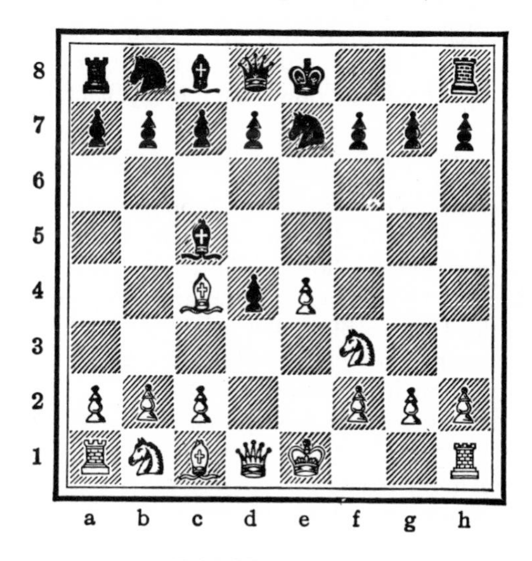

DIAGRAM 25

as it is already attacked by the Bishop c4. The student will, at this stage of his development, not yet know why Black should be so anxious to defend the Pawn f7, considering that he is a Pawn ahead so that the loss of a Pawn would only equalize the forces but would not give White a material advantage. However, later on, when discussing the strategy of the opening, it will become evident that in the position of the diagram Black must, under all circumstances, defend the Pawn f7 as otherwise his game would soon become hopeless on account of the exposed position of his King.

There are only two ways for Black to defend f7. One is to advance the Queen's Pawn to d5, interrupting the diagonal of White's Bishop; the other is to castle, so that the Rook procures the second protection for the Pawn f7 which is needed. It would then not be good for White to capture the Pawn because he would have to give up Knight and Bishop for Rook and one Pawn, which is not a sufficient equivalent.

Of the two ways indicated only the first one is feasible. For if Black castles he gives White an opportunity to institute an attack on the weak Pawn h7 with Knight and Queen against which Black has no satisfactory defense. Play would develop as follows:

(1)	Kt-g5	0-0
(2)	Q-h5	P-h6

This is the only defense against the threat Qxh7 mate. But White's Queen's move involved a double threat. It brought up a third attack on the Pawn f7, and the latter now falls, forcing Black to give up some more material.

(3)	Ktxf7	Rxf7

Black has to sacrifice the exchange. If he moved the Queen, which is attacked by the Knight, he would expose his King to a deadly double check, viz.: (4) Ktxh6++, K-h8 or h7; (5) Kt-f7+ (discovered), K-g8; (6) Q-h8 mate. After giving up his Rook for the Knight on the third move Black has a lost game, for as explained in the previous chapter White can simply exchange all pieces and force the win in the ending with his superior material.

Another square which after castling on the King side is often the mark of attack for the Queen in connection with either Knight or Bishop, is the one immediately in front of the King in the Knight's file. Diagram 26 illustrates several possibilities of this kind.

White, on the move, can play (1) Q-g5, attacking for the second time the Pawn g7 which is only once protected. The threat, however, is not only to win a Pawn, but to win the game, for in taking the Pawn with the Queen White would checkmate Black's King. The only defense at Black's disposal is P-g6, but this move helps only temporarily. White can force the mate within a few moves in different ways. One would be the following:

(2)	Kt-h6+	K-g7

If the King goes to h8 White mates by Q-f6.

(3)	Q-f6+	Kxh6
(4)	B-g5+	K-h5
(5)	P-h3	

and the mate through P-g4 cannot be protected.

Another way would be:

(2)	Q-h6	Pxf5
(3)	B-f6	

and the mate through Q-g7 cannot be protected.

The position of Diagram 26 enables another mating attack for White, demonstrating the possibility of mating with Bishop and Knight in the middle of the game, which occurs oftener than one would be inclined to think. White can play (1) B-f6 instead of Q-g5 as suggested above. Black cannot take the Bishop as White would continue Q-h6 with Q-g7

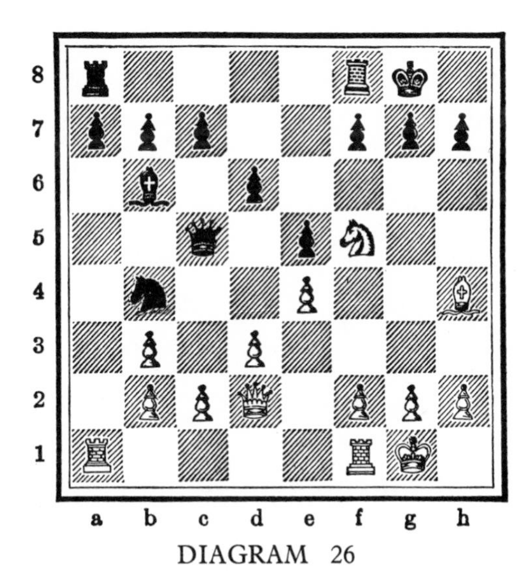

DIAGRAM 26

mate. Neither can Black play P-g6 as then White would mate right away with Kt-h6. The latter mate with Knight and Bishop White can force, even if Black does not move the Pawn g7 but makes some other indifferent move, as for instance Qxc2. White would then make the surprising move Q-h6, allowing Black to take the Queen. In doing so, however, Black again enables the mate Kt-h6.

The only move which Black could try in answer to (1) B-f6 is P-h6, preventing the Queen from occupying g5. Now Qxh6 would not be feasible as after Pxh6 White does not mate with Ktxh6, but leaves the square h7 open to Black's King. However, White wins easily through (2) Ktxh6+. If Black takes the Knight, White mates with Qxh6 and Q-g7. If Black does not take but plays K-h7, White goes back with the Knight to f5, again threatening Q-g5 and Qxg7. (3) . . ., R-g8 is of no avail, as (4) Q-g5 threatens mate of h5 which can only be prevented by either P-g6 or a move with the Rook, after which White mates by either Q-h6 or Qxg7.

It remains to show some examples of the coöperation of Rooks with other pieces. Diagram 27 shows one of the positions in which the beginner is frequently caught. White plays (1) Q-h5, and if Black makes an indifferent move he mates through (2) Qxh7+, Kxh7; (3) R-h5.

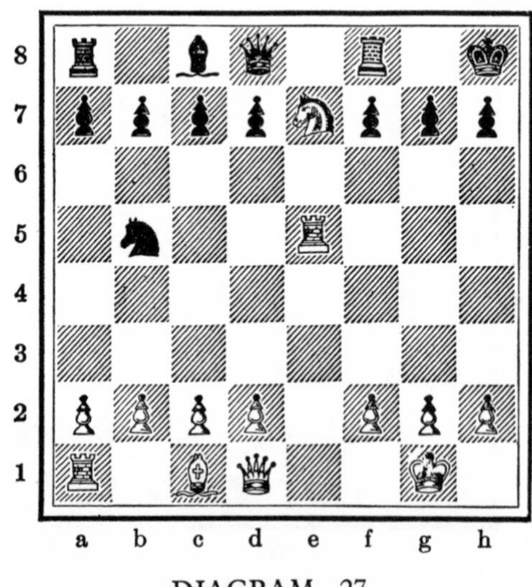

DIAGRAM 27

Black could try to defend himself with (1) . . ., P-g6. White can then continue with (2) Q-h6 and again Black cannot make an indifferent move such as P-d6 for instance, as White would have another mate in two moves, namely (3) R-h5 (threatening Qxh7), Pxh5; (4) Q-f6.

More frequent than the mate with Rook and Knight shown above is one which usually occurs in the end game and which is illustrated in Diagram 28.

White plays Kt-f6+ and Black cannot go with the King into the corner as the Rook would mate him on h7. After K-f8 White draws the game through perpetual check; for after (2) Kt-h7+, K-e8; (3) Kt-f6+ the King must go back to f8 as on d8 he would be mated by R-d7. Consequently White can check the King indefinitely on h7 and f6.

An example for the coöperation of Rook and Bishop is shown in Diagram 29. White plays B-f6, and there is no way for Black to prevent the mate threatened through R-h3 followed by R-h8.

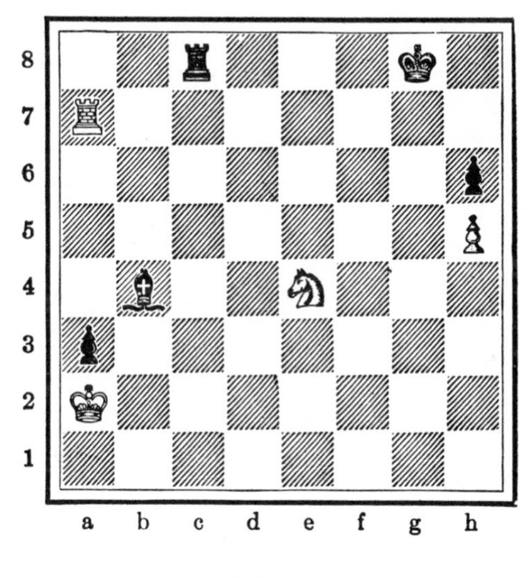

DIAGRAM 28

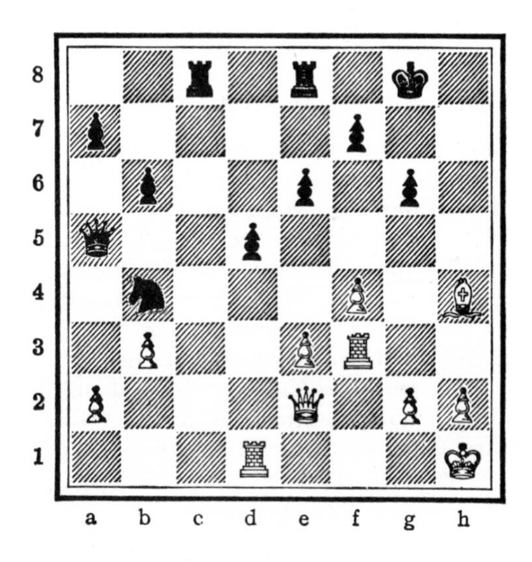

DIAGRAM 29

It is evident that the force of the Rooks will increase as the board gets emptier through the exchange of men, for they will then find more open lines to act in. One of the most important lines for Rooks to occupy is—especially in the ending—the one in which most of the attackable Pawns of the opponent are standing, that is in the majority of cases the

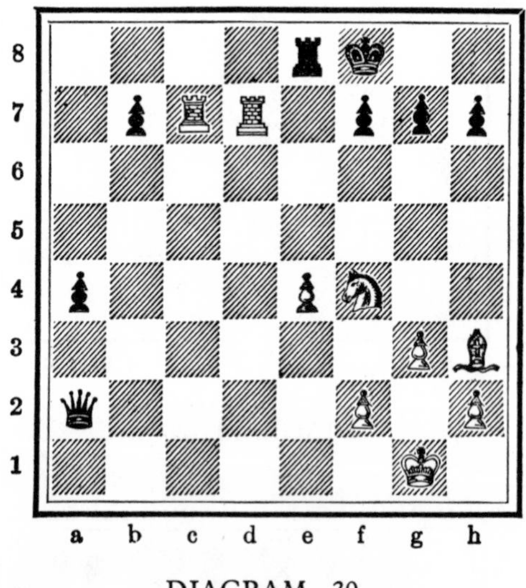

DIAGRAM 30

second or the seventh rank respectively. If both Rooks coöperate with each other in this rank they usually decide the victory within a short time.

Following is an example which is taken from a master game. As far as the material is concerned the players are about even, as the Queen is worth as much as the two Rooks while Knight and Bishop are an approximate equivalent of the Black Rook and the Pawn which Black is ahead. The Pawn a4 is rather dangerous for White, as he needs only three more moves to reach the first rank where he can be promoted into any piece. On the other hand the Rooks doubled in the seventh rank give White so strong an attack on the Black King that he forces the mate before Black succeeds in realizing the advantage of his advanced passed Pawn.

It is White's move. If Black's Queen did not protect the Pawn f7 White would be able to give a mate in five moves, thus: (1) Rxf7+, K-g8; (2) Rxg7+, K-h8 (not K-f8 on account of Rc7-f7 mate); (3) Rxh7+, K-g8; (4) R-g7+ and Kt-g6 mate.

Therefore, White will try to interrupt the diagonal in which the Queen defends the threat, and he can do so by (1) Kt-d5. Black being unable to keep f7 protected, must defend g7 or h7, or he will be mated. In the game in question Black played Q-a1+; (2) K-g2, P-a3. After (3) Rxf7+, K-g8 it would not be good for White to take g7, giving up

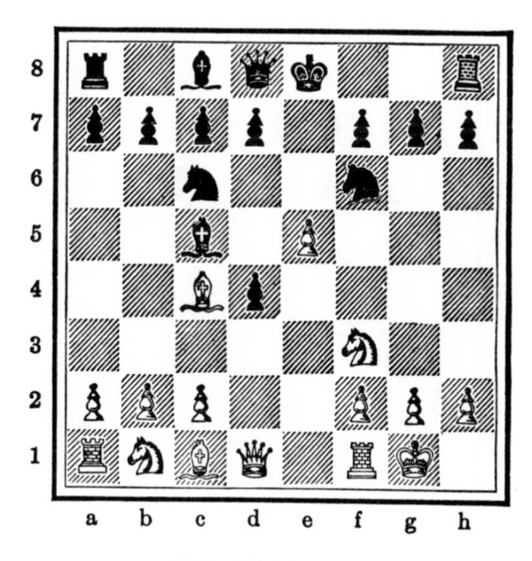

DIAGRAM 31

the two Rooks for the Queen, as he would then have no more attack while Black still has the dangerous Pawn in the a-line. If possible he will rather interrupt again the diagonal of Black's Queen. This suggests the move (4) Kt-f6+. After Pxf6 White's Rooks are at last free to act unmolested in the seventh rank, and they do it with deadly effect. White forces the mate through (5) R-g7+, K-h8; (6) Rxh7+, K-g8; (7) Rh7-g7+, K-h8; (8) B-f5! Now R-g4 is threatened followed by R-h7 mate, and Black has no defense.

In the opening and in the middle game the main threat of a Rook is the "pinning" of a hostile piece. What is meant by this is illustrated in Diagram 31. Supposing Black, to save his Knight f6 which White has just attacked by P-e5, plays Kt-g4 and after (2) P-h3 takes the Pawn e5 with the Knight g4, then White wins a piece by (3) Ktxe5, Ktxe5; (4) R-e1. This move "pins" Black's Knight to his place as the King would be exposed to White's Rook if the Knight moved. (4) . . ., P-d6 or Q-e7 is not a sufficient defense, for White continues with (5) P-f4.

Pieces that can be used for pinning a hostile man are, apart from the Rooks, the Queen and the Bishops; in fact pinning is the main activity of a Bishop throughout the game. Right after the first few moves one of the Bishops, as a rule, finds an opportunity to pin a hostile Knight. For instance: (1) P-e4, P-e5; (2) Kt-f3, Kt-c6; (3) B-b5 and as soon as

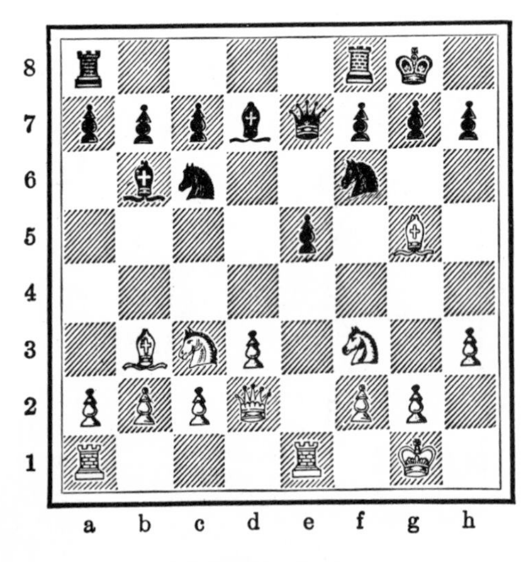

DIAGRAM 32

the Pawn d7 moves in order to give an outlet to the Bishop c8, the Knight c6 is pinned. Or: (1) P-d4, P-d5; (2) Kt-f3, Kt-f6; (3) P-c4, P-e6; (4) B-g5 and the Knight f6 is pinned, as the Queen would be lost if the Knight moved.

The disadvantage arising from having a piece pinned is often that the opponent might be able to concentrate more men to attack the piece which is pinned than can be gathered for defense. The position of Diagram 32 will serve as an illustration.

Two of Black's men are pinned, namely, the Knight f6 and the Pawn e5, and of both pins White can take advantage.

The Pawn e5 is attacked twice and defended twice. White cannot take Pawn, as he would lose Knight and Rook but would get for it only Knight and Pawn. However, he can win the Pawn by playing (1) P-d4. This attacks the Pawn for the third time and although Black can defend him for the third time with R-e8, the defense is not serviceable as Black would lose Pawn, Knight and Queen for Pawn, Knight and Rook.

P-e4 in answer to P-d4 would not help either; for on e4 the Pawn is twice attacked and only once protected as the Knight f6 cannot be counted as protection on account of his being pinned by the Bishop g5. All White needs to do is to take the Knight f6 first and then to capture the Pawn e4.

It remains to examine whether in answer to (1) P-d4 Black can take the Pawn with either Bishop or Knight. Apparently this is possible as the Pawn d4 is protected only by the Knight f3 and the Queen. Indeed, the combination would be correct if the Bishop d7 were sufficiently protected. As it is White wins a piece in the following way:

(1) P-d4	Bxd4
(2) Ktxd4	Ktxd4
(3) Qxd4	Pxd4
(4) Rxe7	Pxc3

Up to this move an even exchange of pieces has taken place, but now Black loses the Bishop which is attacked by White's Rook, because White can remove the Knight which protects the Bishop.

(5) Bxf6	Pxf6
(6) Rxd7, etc.	

Instead of playing (1) P-d4 and taking advantage of the fact that the Pawn e5 is pinned, White can direct his attack against the other Black man which is pinned, namely the Knight f6. He can play (1) Kt-d5 and thereby attack the Queen and at the same time the Knight f6 for the second time. It will not be evident to the beginner that White can derive any advantage from this double attack, as Black can answer either Q-d6 or Q-d8 keeping his Knight twice protected. Indeed, White does not gain anything on f6, the square itself upon which the pin is effected, but he uses the pin to force an opening into the chain of Pawns which protects Black's King by exchanging on f6, compelling Black to retake with the Pawn g7. The advantage resulting from this break in Black's Pawn position will be explained later on when discussing the strategy of the middle-game.

SACRIFICING

A player is said to *sacrifice* if he allows a certain amount of his forces to be captured without recapturing himself an equivalent amount of his opponent's forces. He will not, of course, knowingly do so unless he expects to obtain some other advantage which will at least compensate for his loss of material. Such compensation can only be afforded by a superiority of the *position.* Inasmuch as a position can only be considered superior if it enables the mating of the opposing King or the obtaining of an advantage in material which will secure a win in the ending, it is evident that in sacrificing a player really never intends to give up more than he gets, but that on the contrary he expects to gain more than he loses. In other words, a sacrifice, if correct, is a sacrifice only *temporarily*, and very soon yields either the same, if not more material, or an attack on the King to which the latter falls victim.

The less evident the way is in which a player recovers the material

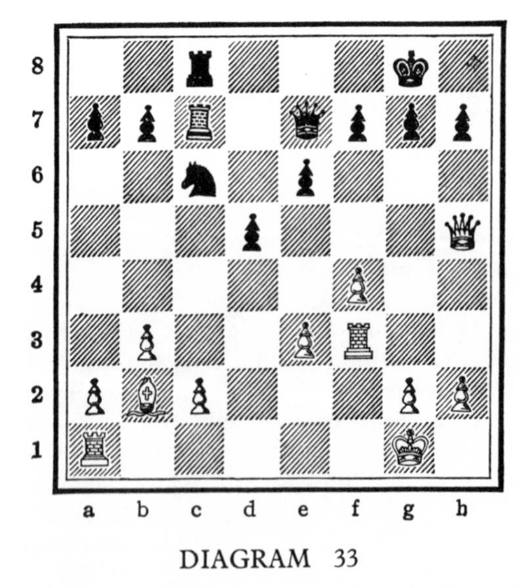

DIAGRAM 33

sacrificed or realizes an equivalent advantage the more beautiful the sacrifice is considered. If the effect of a sacrifice is a direct mating attack on the King, it is as a rule not difficult to foresee as long as the typical mating positions are known to the player, most of which have been discussed in the previous chapter. The following diagrams illustrate examples of such sacrifices which occur fairly often in actual games.

In Diagram 33, White on the move can play for a similar mate as the one explained in the discussion of Diagram 29 by placing his Rook on g3. The best protection against Rxg7 which Black has at his disposal is P-f6. But if he does not know the mating position illustrated in Diagram 29 he is liable to play P-g6, and then White forces the mate by sacrificing his Queen on h7.

(1) R-g3	P-g6
(2) Qxh7+	Kxh7
(3) R-h3+	K-g8
(4) R-h8±	

Black could have prolonged the agony one move by interposing his Queen on h4 on the third move.

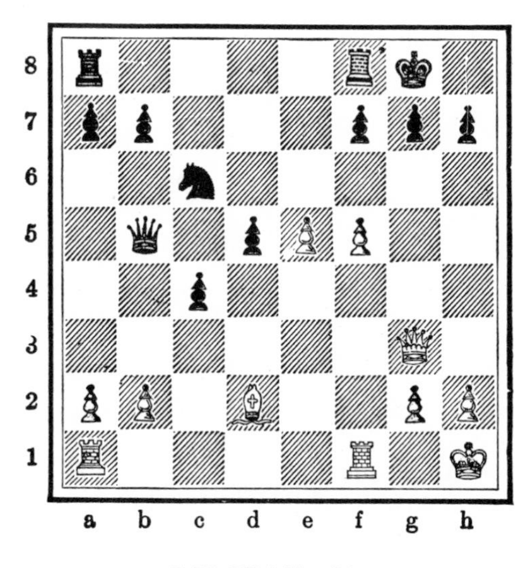

DIAGRAM 34

In the position of Diagram 34 White institutes a mating attack by (1) P-f6. The only move to protect the mate on g7 is P-g6. It will then be White's desire to enter with his Queen on h6 again threatening the checkmate on g7. He will, therefore, play either Q-f4 or Q-g5. Black has no other way to defend himself against White's threat than by K-h8 followed by R-g8. But after K-h8; Q-h6, R-g8 White plays R-f3 and Black is unable to prevent White from sacrificing his Queen on h7 and mating by R-h3.

If Black's Queen were standing on c5 instead of b5 he could avert the mate by moving the Rook f8 and playing the Queen to f8 thereby protecting g7.

The mate with Rook and Knight demonstrated by the position of Diagram 28 is liable to occur in several variations of the play which might result from the following situation:

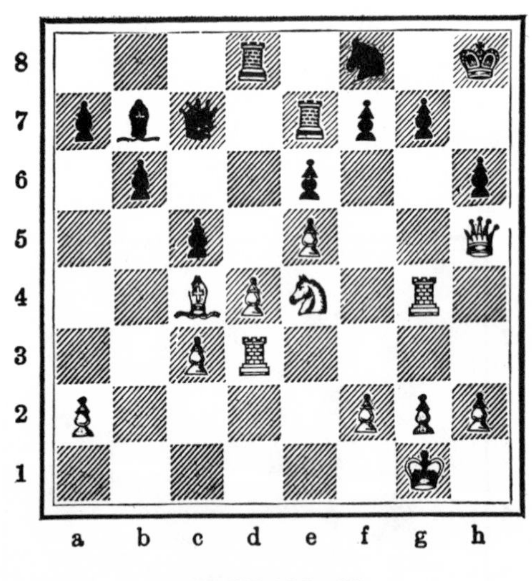

DIAGRAM 35

White starts his mating attack with (1) Kt-f6. This threatens the sacrifice of the Queen on h6 followed by R-g8 mate. White's Knight move can hardly be called a sacrifice as it is quite evident that Black cannot take the Knight on account of Qxh6+, Kt-h7; Q-g7 mate. The only way to parry White's threat is (1) . . ., Kt-g6. However, this helps only momentarily as White continues (2) R-h3 threatening Q-g5, Rxh6+ and Qxh6 mate, a threat against which Black has no defense. White can very nearly force the mate by sacrificing his Queen on h6 instead of the Rook. But after (3) Qxh6, Pxh6; (4) Rxh6+, K-g7; (5) R-h7+, K-f8; (6) R-h8+ Black does not take the Rook as White would like him to do to enable the mate R-g8, but he goes back to g7 with the King and White could not do any better than draw by perpetual check on h7 and h8.

In the position of Diagram 36 White can make an attack which will recall somewhat the play shown in connection with Diagram 25. (1) Kt-g5 would not lead to anything, as Black could defend himself by

P-g6 or P-h6. White has a much more direct way to attack the black King. This is by the sacrifice (1) Bxh7+. After Kxh7; (2) Kt-g5+, K-g8; (3) Q-h5 Black can protect the mate only by sacrificing his Queen for White's Knight. For (3) . . ., R-e8 with the view to escape with the King to e7 via f8 if attacked by Q-h7 and Q-h8 would be

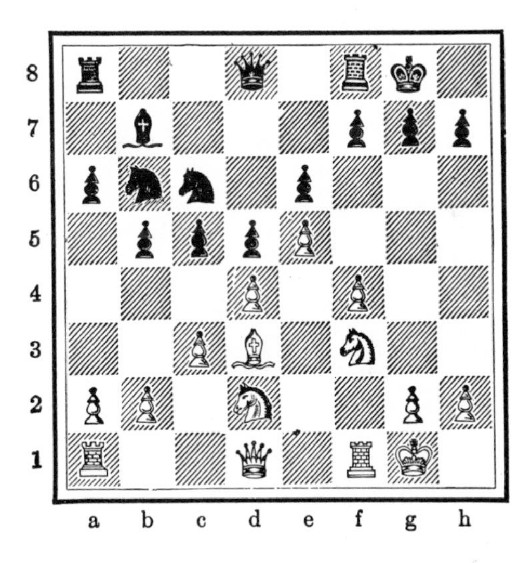

DIAGRAM 36

rendered futile by White through (4) Qxf7+, K-h8; (5) Q-h5+, K-g8; (6) Q-h7+, K-f8; (7) Q-h8+, K-e7; (8) Qxg7 mate. Before making the sacrifice of the Bishop White will, of course, have to make sure that Black cannot save himself by evading altogether the attack which is threatened through Q-h5. Black could, indeed, avoid this variation by going with the King to g6 on the second move instead of g8. But in this case too White has a winning continuation. He would play (3) Q-g4 threatening to win Black's Queen by the discovered check Ktxe6. If Black moves the Queen, then White gives the discovered check in any case forcing the King to h7 and leading over to the variation which was originally intended. If, on the other hand, Black tried (3) . . ., P-f5, attacking White's Queen and thereby rendering the discovered check ineffective, White would first take the Pawn en passant and after (4) Pxf6, Kxf6 the Queen mates on e6.

Frequently a sacrifice is brought to maintain a pin which is bound to yield a piece in return sooner or later. The position of Diagram 37 is typical for cases of this kind. Supposing Black plays (1) . . ., P-h6; (2) B-h4, P-g5 to free himself of the pinning Bishop. Then White can sacrifice the Knight f3 for the two black Pawns and thereby maintain the pin with the threat to regain the Knight immediately through Kt-d5. The ensuing play could be the following: (3) Ktxg5, Pxg5; (4) Bxg5, Bxc3; (5) Pxc3. Now White threatens to play P-f4 and Pxe5 opening the line of his Rook and thereby attacking the pinned Knight for the

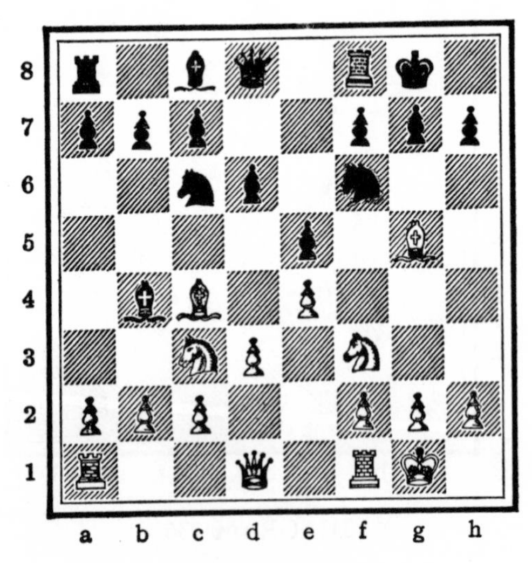

DIAGRAM 37

second time. This threat cannot be effectively countered. Black could try to unpin the Knight by (5) . . . , K-g7; (6) P-f4, Q-e8. Indeed, Black saves his Knight in this way, but the exposed position of his King leads to a speedy disaster. For instance: (7) Pxe5, Kt-h7; (8) B-f6+, Ktxf6; (9) Pxf6+, K-h7; (10) Q-h5+, K-g8; (11) Q-g6+, K-h8; (12) Q-g7±. Black could not take White's Queen on the 11th move because the Pawn f7 was pinned by the Bishop c4.

If Black had moved his King to g8 or g6 on the 8th move instead of taking the Bishop f6, White would have forced the mate by sacrificing his Rook on f5, thereby cutting off the Bishop c8 and giving his Queen access to the square g4.

Sacrifices with the view to utilizing a pin occur in various other versions which are essentially different from the one illustrated above. Following are typical examples of the three most frequent cases.

three times attacked and three times protected so that White cannot take him as now the pin of the Rook resulting from Ktxf7, Ktxf7; Qxf7, Rxf7 does not lead to anything, the square e8 being protected by the Queen. However, White can force the win by (2) Ra1-e1, threatening again the sacrifice of f7, as he now controls the square e8 twice. If

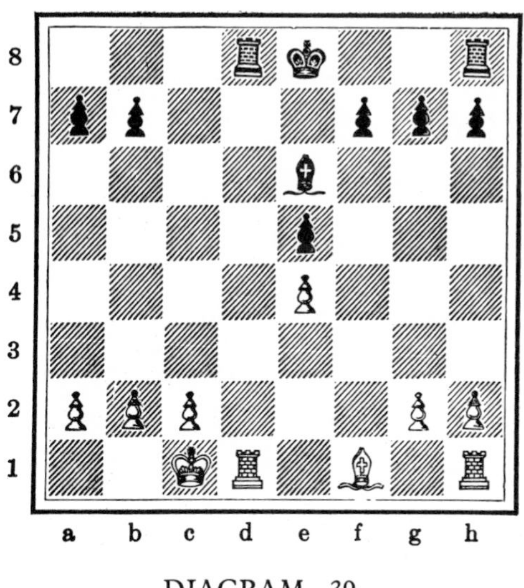

DIAGRAM 39

Black replies (2) . . ., Q-f6, protecting f7 for the fourth time and thereby making impossible White's sacrifice on that point, White continues with (3) R-e8. This threatens Rxf8+, Kxf8; Ktxh7+ winning the Queen. Black cannot defend himself with Q-g6 on account of (4) B-d3 followed by Bxh7+ and Rxf8, etc., nor can he play (3) . . ., Q-f4 on account of P-g3 followed by Qxd6, attacking the defenseless Rook f8.

A sacrifice with the view to enabling a mating attack through the coöperation of Rooks and Bishop somewhat similar to the examples discussed in the previous chapter is possible in the position of Diagram 41 which occurred in a Tournament game in London in which the author conducted the black men.

Black's combination starts with the sacrifice of the Queen on f3. After (1) . . ., Qxf3; (2) Pxf3, B-h3+; (3) K-g1 White's King is held in an immobile position by the Black Bishop and a check with one of Black's Rooks in the g-file would be deadly.

However, White can, for a while, protect himself against all mating

In the position of Diagram 38 Black must not take th
although he can protect the Knight with B-f5 in case White
with R-e1. The way in which White would obtain the adva
this:

(1)	R-e1	B-f5
(2)	Rxe4	Bxe4
(3)	R-e1	

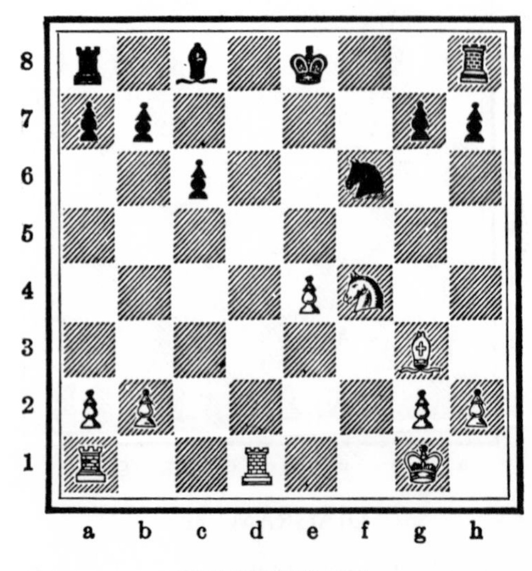

DIAGRAM 38

Through sacrificing one Rook for the Knight White has freed the square e1 for the other Rook who now pins the Black Bishop without Black being able to protect it.

The position of Diagram 39 is somewhat related to that of Diagram 38, as far as the possibility of a sacrifice for the sake of a pin is concerned. If White plays B-b5+ Black must not interpose his Bishop, for White will give up his Rook for the Bishop in order to force the Rook d8 into a pinned position and then he will win the Rook by R-d1.

In the position of Diagram 40 there is also a possibility of a sacrifice with the view to pin a piece that defends a certain threat as long as it is mobile. White plays (1) Q-d5, and Black dares not take White's Knight with his Queen for White would continue (2) Qxf7+, Rxf7; (3) R-e8±.

What Black could try is (1) Kt-h6. The Pawn f7 would then be attempts of Black. If Black continued (3) . . ., R-e6, White would take the Pawn d3 with the Queen thereby defending the mate R-g6. After giving up his Queen for one of Black's Rooks, White would still have an advantage in material.

The correct way to carry on the attack is (3) . . ., Ra8-e8, as then

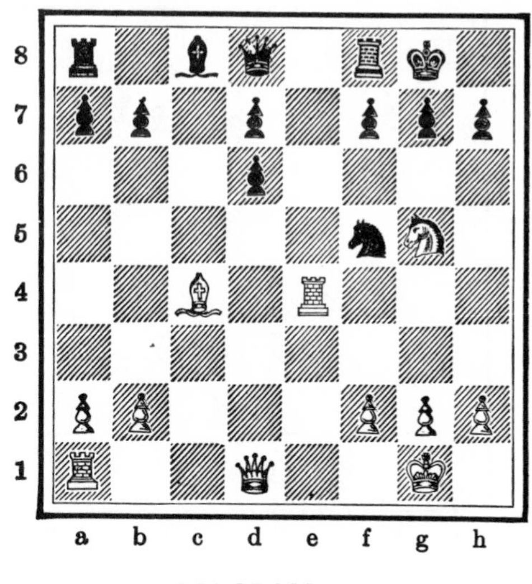

DIAGRAM 40

White cannot take the Pawn d3 on account of R-e1+; Q-f1, Rxf1+; Rxf1, R-e6 and R-g6 mate.

The main threat of Black's third move is R-e6-g6 mate. Another threat is P-d2 followed by R-e1+. The only way for White to defend himself is (4) P-f4. If now P-d2, then (5) P-f3, R-e1+; (6) K-f2 affords a sufficient protection. And if (4) . . ., Re8-e6, then (5) P-f5 prevents the Rook from going to g6.

However, by repeating the mating threat with (5) . . ., Re6-e4, which forces White to protect g4 by (6) P-f3 Black opens the second rank for a combined assault of the Rooks similar to the one illustrated by Diagram 30. What makes matters worse for White is that with (6) . . ., R-g2+ he is forced into the line of the Bishop h3 so that he is exposed to a discovered check. After (7) K-f1, Rxb2 discovered check; (8) K-g1, Re4-e2 White must give up his Queen for the Rook immediately, as otherwise Black would mate in four moves by R-g2+, K-f1, Rxh2+, K-g1, Rb2-g2+; K-f1, Rxh1 ±.

Although White is still ahead in material after (9) Qxe2, Rxe2 he cannot avoid the loss of the game on account of the continued threat which Black exerts by the coöperation of his Rook and his Bishop. The only move which would save the Rook a1 from getting lost through R-g2+, followed by a discovered check with simultaneous attack of the

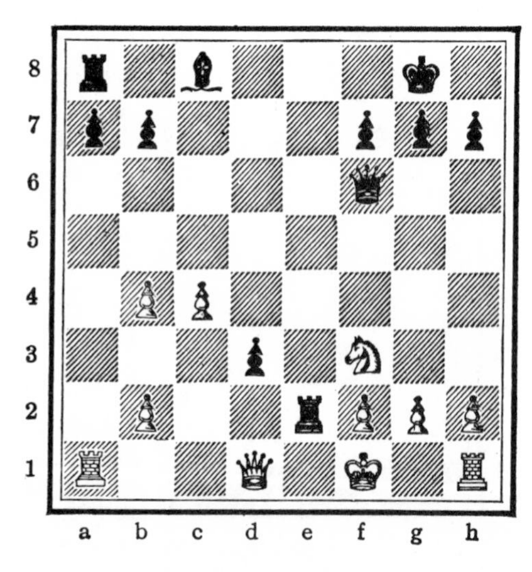

DIAGRAM 41

Rook by Black's Rook would be (10) R-d1 with the idea of protecting the Rook with the King thus (10) . . ., R-g2+; (11) K-f1, R-d2; (12) K-e1; but this plan fails as Black checkmates with (12) . . ., R-e2.

A mating position which has not been discussed up to now but which occurs frequently enough in the actual game to warrant its special mention is one in which the King is deprived of all mobility by his own men who surround him and in which a hostile Knight can check the King. Diagram 42 offers an example.

White on the move can force the mate by (1) R-d8, a very surprising sacrifice indeed, for not only can Black take the Rook with either Queen or Rook but he can also take White's Queen. In the latter case, however, he would be mated in two moves by (2) Rxe8+, Q-g8; (3) Kt-f7. This is one example of the "throttled mate" by the Knight. Another one, which is really the typical one, occurs if Black takes the Rook instead of the Queen. The mating process then is: (2) Kt-f7+, K-g8; (3) Kt-h6 double check, K-h8; (4) Q-g8+, Rxg8; (5) Kt-f7±.

White could not have played Q-g8+ right on the second move because then Black would have taken the Queen with the King, while he could not do so with White's Knight on h6.

Sacrifices made with the view of a direct mating attack are, as a rule, the easiest to figure out, as there is no guesswork connected with them.

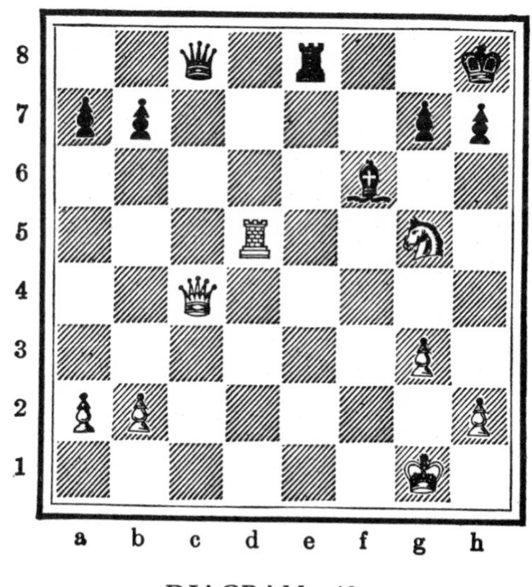

DIAGRAM 42

In those cases the player does not face the question as to whether the position attained after the sacrifice will be strong enough to insure a gain of material at least equivalent to the amount of material sacrificed, a question which to answer correctly sometimes requires a good deal of instinct trained by experience; all that is necessary is to ascertain whether the opponent can be mated in a definite number of moves or not. If the mate cannot be clearly foreseen, the sacrifice must not be made. The possibility of a sacrifice with consequent forced mate is always indicated if a greatly superior force is available for attack at the part of the board where the opposing King is located. An example is offered by the position reproduced on page ii. This position occurred in a game between Sir G. A. Thomas of London and the author. Black has just played Q-e7 in order to protect the mate which was threatened by Ktxf6+ followed by Qxh7. If in the position of the diagram White played Kt-f6+, Black would retake with the Pawn, thereby protecting the Pawn h7 with his Queen. However,

White can force the mate with a neat Queen's sacrifice which drives Black's King right into the arms of the remaining White pieces. Play continues as follows:

(1)	Qxh7+	Kxh7
(2)	Ktxf6++	K-h6

The King cannot go to h8 on account of Kt-g6 mate. White now continually checks Black's King in such a manner that he has only one square to go to until he is finally driven to the first rank, all White pieces participating in the chase.

(3) Kte5-g4+

In answer to Ktf6-g4+ Black would play K-h5; (4) B-g6+, K-h4; (5) P-g3+, K-h3 and there is no mate.

(3)	. . .	K-g5
(4)	P-h4+	K-f4
(5)	P-g3+	K-f3
(6)	B-e2+	K-g2
(7)	R-h2+	K-g1
(8)	K-d2 mate.	

White could have forced the mate in seven instead of eight moves by playing (6) K-f1, or (6) o-o, for there was no protection against (7) Kt-h2.

III

GENERAL PRINCIPLES OF CHESS STRATEGY

In reading the chapter on "Elementary Tactics" the beginner will have obtained a fair idea of the value of the different pieces and he will have gained an insight into the possibilities of their coöperation. However, the fundamental principle of Chess strategy, the method of developing the inherent powers of the men so that they may be able to do all the work possible for them, will still be a secret to him.

At the beginning of the game the Knights are the only pieces which are able to move, and consequently the other pieces are worthless until openings have been created for them by Pawn moves. Now, the first thing the beginner should try to keep in mind is that only such Pawn moves can be good as open lines for their fellow pieces or obstruct lines of opposing men. The reason is this:

In any hand to hand fight evidently that player will get the better of it who has more pieces ready for action on the battlefield. When examining the typical positions discussed in the previous chapter the fact will strike the observant reader that the winning player always has a decided superiority of forces at his disposal where the actual fight is going on, so that in some cases he can even sacrifice a great amount of them and still have enough left for the final onslaught against the King. The same holds good in combinations where lesser objects than the King are fought for; the player who has more pieces ready to take part in the struggle will emerge victorious; the player who attacks with less pieces than the opponent has on the spot for defense, cannot hope to succeed.

The important point, therefore, is to place the pieces so that they will be in readiness for concentration on whatever part of the board they are needed.

Moreover, it will be important to place the pieces on such favorable squares in the shortest possible time—meaning with the smallest number of moves—as wasting moves on maneuvers which do not further the mobilization of the troops will give the opponent an opportunity to gather a superior force somewhere on the board and make an attack with the best chance in the world to succeed before reënforcements can be brought up.

With this aim in mind the beginner will readily see that it is by no means immaterial which Pawn moves are made in the opening. The fact that a Pawn move opens an outlet for a piece is not sufficient. If possible Pawn moves will have to be found which enable the development of more than one piece for they will lead to an advantage in the mobilization unless the opponent, too, hastens the development of his pieces by equally good Pawn moves.

The only Pawn moves which fit this description are moves with the King's or Queen's Pawns as they open lines for Queen and Bishop—apart from an additional square for the Knight—while the other Pawns cannot free the way for more than one piece. Whether the move with the King's Pawn or the Queen's Pawn is better when beginning the game is impossible to say. In neither case can it be proved that White can obtain an advantage which is sufficient to win the game. With correct play on both sides it can be only White who gains an advantage, for he has the first move and so he is one move ahead of Black in the development as long as he does not waste any time on maneuvers which do not increase the mobility of his pieces.

By the mobility of a piece is meant the number of squares accessible to it. A Bishop or a Rook which stands in an unobstructed file is obviously worth more than one whose sphere of action is limited on account of his way being blocked. This does not mean, however, that a Bishop or a Knight to whom, at a certain moment, three or four squares are accessible, is more valuable than a Rook who at the same moment can go only to one or two squares; for a few moves later the Rook might be in possession of his full freedom while the action of the Bishop or the Knight might be hampered. It is, therefore, best to value the pieces according to their latent strength, that is, the strength which is likely to show in the ending after all temporary obstructions have been removed. The comparative values given for the different men on page 24 will serve as good guide in most cases. It is not advisable though to give up a minor piece for three Pawns or two minor pieces for a Rook and one Pawn as long as Queens and minor pieces are on the board, as with a piece ahead the opponent mostly succeeds in winning through a direct attack against the King before the superiority of Pawns becomes dangerous.

In trying to place the pieces on squares where they have as much mobility as possible individual thought is required with each new game as it depends altogether upon the moves of the opponent which lines can be opened for Bishops, Rooks and Queen and where a good field of action can be secured for the Knights. However, it is possible to give a few rules which common sense tells us must hold good in the majority of games if both players play well. Of course, if a player makes bad moves in the opening, that is, moves which do not aim at a speedy mobilization of all pieces, then the opponent may soon have a chance to win the game with moves which are not in accordance with those common sense rules either but which force an immediate issue in a maneuver of a kind that ordinarily does not occur in an opening but is characteristic of the middle game. This is a point which the majority of Chess players overlook. They argue that—granted the value of general principles of strategy, which will greatly help to build up a safe position—cases occur in which a move may win which is not according to principles, and that, therefore, following the trend of a certain combination which seems profitable, is advisable even if the general principles are violated.

Even a Chess master once said, that generalities are of no use in Chess and that it is necessary to figure out every move in all variations to which it may lead to make sure that the move is good. As an example he offered the following opening: (1) P-f3, P-e5; (2) P-g4. Now, he asks, should Black omit to give the checkmate with Q-h4 because it is against the general principles to bring out the Queen at an early stage of the game?

The shallowness of this argument is obvious. The reason for the general rule that the Queen should not come out too soon is that she is liable to be attacked by the minor pieces of the opponent so that she has to move again and again and time is lost which could be used for the development of other pieces. Of course, if the opponent does not develop his pieces, the Queen may often come out without danger and she may do a lot of harm before she can be driven away.

In formulating general strategical principles it is, then, assumed that both players will follow them, and it is taken for granted that if one player deviates from these principles and thereby weakens himself at some point, the other player is expected to exact the full penalty for this deviation with any means at his disposal. It will always be found that these means are also indicated by the general principles if only their meaning is intelligently applied to the position in question.

As was stated before, the point of greatest importance in the opening is to develop the pieces without loss of time, that is, to place them on squares where they have as much mobility as possible without making any move which retards this development. There are different ways in which the development may be retarded, and which consequently must be avoided. For instance, no Pawn move should be made which is not absolutely necessary to open a line for a piece; or, no piece should move twice as long as there are pieces which have not yet moved at all; or, no piece should be developed to a square from which the opponent can drive it away at the same time furthering his own development; or, the right of castling should not be foregone by moving the King or by any other way, as castling develops a Rook and places the King in safety with one move while more moves are required to the same end if castling is not possible, and so on.

The beginner who makes this great principle of development quite clear to himself has made the most difficult step on the way to mastership. The grasp of the far reaching influence of the mobility of the pieces in the opening upon the further development of the whole game is really what distinguishes the master from the average player.

Of course, it would be too difficult for the beginner to find out for himself what squares are the most favorable for the different pieces; at any rate, it would take him a long time to gain that knowledge by experience. Fortunately, the experience of the masters of several generations is accessible to us and so it is possible to expedite considerably the process by which the mind of the student is adapted to the tactics required in every game of Chess to carry out the principle of speedy development. To a great extent these tactics, too, can be simply explained from the point of view of giving the pieces their utmost mobility so that they will be readily understood by the reader who has followed the arguments given in the foregoing pages.

There is a considerable difference in the constellation of the pieces depending on whether the game is opened with the King's or the Queen's Pawn. These two openings shall therefore be treated separately. All other openings are related to one of the above main branches and need little additional discussion.

KING'S PAWN OPENINGS

After (1) P-e4, P-e5 the only Pawn which both players have to move to enable the development of all pieces is the Queen's Pawn, which obstructs the Queen's Bishop. Of course, it would also be possible to secure an outlet for the Queen's Bishop by advancing the Queen's Knight's Pawn one step; but in the long diagonal the Bishop is ordinarily not so well posted as the development of the Queen's Knight to his most natural square, that is c3 or c6 respectively, would block the way of the Bishop. The Queen's Knight is best placed in the c-file because on the edge of the board, in the a-file, he has less mobility; less squares are accessible to him. In order to place him in the d-file it would be necessary to move the d-Pawn, and as this would also give an opening to the Queen's Bishop the move of the Queen's Knight's Pawn is superfluous.

Before moving the Queen's Pawn the players will have to make sure that in advancing him they will not block the way of any piece. Consequently, White will not play P-d3 on his second move. He will first develop the King's Bishop. Of course, he will not place him on d3, obstructing the Queen's Pawn and thereby the Queen's Bishop. Neither will he play B-b5, as Black could drive him away from there immediately with P-c6, opening another diagonal for the Queen. The choice between the remaining squares, e2 and c4, is not difficult. On e2 the Bishop would be in the way of the Queen and his way would soon be blocked by the King's Knight, who for similar reasons to those given for the move of the Queen's Knight will go to f3 in preference to other squares. Therefore, the only move to be considered in case the King's Bishop is played at this early stage of the game, is B-c4.

White is not forced to develop this Bishop on the second move by any means. He could either play (2) Kt-f3 or (2) Kt-c3 or (2) P-d4. The objection to the latter move, however, is that after (2) . . ., Pxd4; (3) Qxd4 the white Queen is exposed to the attack of the Knight b8, which means loss of time. Kt-f3 or Kt-c3 are probably preferable to B-c4 on the second move, because it is certain that the Knights will not find any better squares on their initial move. The Bishop, however, may have an occasion to be used on b5 instead of on c4, and it is a good thing, generally speaking, to keep the option of moving a piece to different squares as long as it is compatible with the other requirements of the position.

That the Bishop may be used to advantage on b5 will be seen from the following variation. Supposing White plays (2) Kt-f3. Then the Pawn e5 is attacked. The only sensible protection is (2) . . ., Kt-c6; for P-f6 does not come into consideration, as it is a Pawn move which does not add anything to the development of the pieces; P-d6 blocks the Bishop f8; B-d6 obstructs the Queen's Pawn and Q-f6 or Q-e7 hinders the development of the Knight or the Bishop respectively. Now, it can readily be seen that after (2) . . ., Kt-c6 White may want to place his King's Bishop on b5, for with this move he repeats indirectly his attack on the King's Pawn through the threat to remove the protecting Knight. It is true, that this threat needs no attention as long as White's King's Pawn is not protected (for instance: (3) . . ., Kt-f6; (4) Bxc6, Pd7xc6; (5) Ktxe5, Q-d4 attacking Knight and Pawn at the same time and thereby regaining the Pawn) but as soon as White has defended the Pawn—with P-d3 may be—the Bishop b5 is at work and Black must seek additional protection for the Pawn e5.

If White, on his second move, plays B-c4, he attacks the Pawn f7. This Pawn is protected by Black's King and so he need not be defended any further; but Black must be on the alert against a concentration of some more white men on f7. White could try (3) Q-f3 or Q-h5. However, Black would then have time to defend himself with Kt-f6 or Q-e7 respectively.

Therefore, on the second move, Black may make any developing move; he could, of course, play (2) . . ., Kt-f6, preventing White's Queen from going to h5, but this is unnecessary, as Q-h5 would be a very bad move, placing the Queen on a square from which she is bound to be chased away very soon. For instance: (2) . . ., B-c5; (3) Q-h5, Q-e7 (not P-g6 on account of Qxe5 attacking the King and the Rook at the same time). Now, whatever White plays, he will have to retire again with his Queen as soon as Black attacks her with Kt-f6, and so he loses his birthright of attack; for it will be Black who is a move ahead in the development instead of White, as it ought to be.

If both players refrain from premature attack the game might develop as follows: (2) B-c4, B-c5; (3) Kt-f3, Kt-c6; (4) P-d3, Kt-f6; (5) Kt-c3, P-d6; (6) o-o, o-o; (7) B-g5. This move is the first one with which White trespasses the "frontier" which may be said to run in the openings of all games between the fourth and fifth ranks of the board. The Bishops are the only pieces for whom there is a field of action in the opponent's camp early in the game. They pin a hostile Knight and thereby exert a certain pressure on the opponent who naturally does not like to see any of his pieces deprived of its mobility. The fact that Black can drive White's Bishop away with P-h6 does not lead to any loss of time for White, for the Bishop can retire to h4, still maintaining the pin, while Black has not furthered his development by his Pawn move; in fact, he has somewhat compromised his position and as explained by the discussion of the position of Diagram 37 the advance of the Pawn g7 to g5 cannot follow without the risk that White will uphold the pin even at the cost of a piece and obtain an overwhelming attack.

That the move P-h6 creates a weakness even if it is not followed up by P-g5 will be demonstrated later on in the discussion of the middle game. The correct answer to White's seventh move is easily founp with the help of the principle of development. If White did not threaten anything Black would certainly think of nothing else than the development of his Queen's Bishop, the only minor piece which has not yet moved. Therefore, the first thing Black should consider in countering the threat involved in White's last move is a protection with a move of the Queen's Bishop. White's threat is (8) Kt-d5, attacking the Knight f6 for the second time. Although the Knight is twice protected, Black will naturally endeavour to prevent an accumulation of hostile pieces on the point f6, and he can do that indeed very easily by playing (7) . . ., B-e6 with a view toward capturing the Knight if he should move to d5.

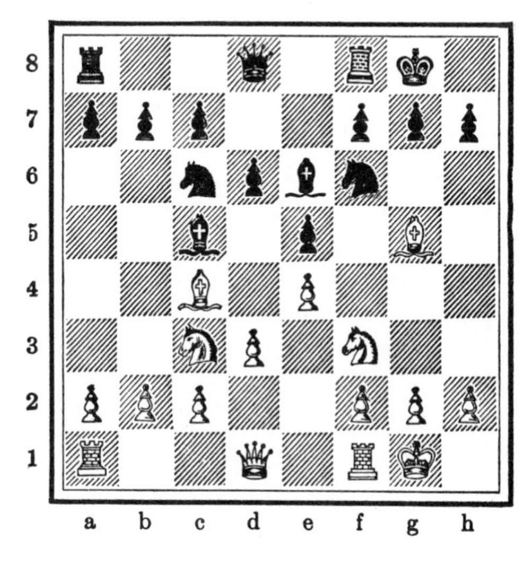

DIAGRAM 43

The exchange (8) Kt-d5, Bxd5; (9) Bxd5 is manifestly not desirable for White, as it does not improve in any way the mobility of his men. On the contrary, White loses a move, as the result of the maneuver is only a change of location of the King's Bishop who was already developed while the principle of speedy development demands that no piece should be moved twice in the opening until *all* pieces are developed.

Unless Black's move involves a threat which needs immediate attention White should consider only such moves as will secure a possibility of development for his Rooks, that is maneuvers which are liable to produce an open file somewhere on the board. This can only be done by the exchange of a Pawn and as the only Pawn within easy reach is the Pawn e5 the files which are liable to be opened first are the d-file and the f-file. In the position of the Diagram it is not easy to find a way of opening either file mentioned without elaborate preparation. P-d4 cannot be played before the square d4 is three times controlled by White and if White tries to accomplish this by (8) Kt-e2, Black spoils White's plan by Bxc4 without being bothered by the threat Kt-d5 which existed as long as the Knight was posted on c3. If, on the other hand, White exchanges the Bishop first on e6 he helps Black's development by opening the f-file for his Rook. To avoid these alternatives White could withdraw the Bishop c4 to b3 and then play Kt-e2 followed by P-c3 and P-d4. But this maneuver involves two moves with pieces which are already developed and it is therefore preferable to place the Rook a1, who has to be developed, right away in the Queen's file and then to proceed as suggested above. In other words, White does probably best to play (8) Q-d2 and (9) Ra1-d1.

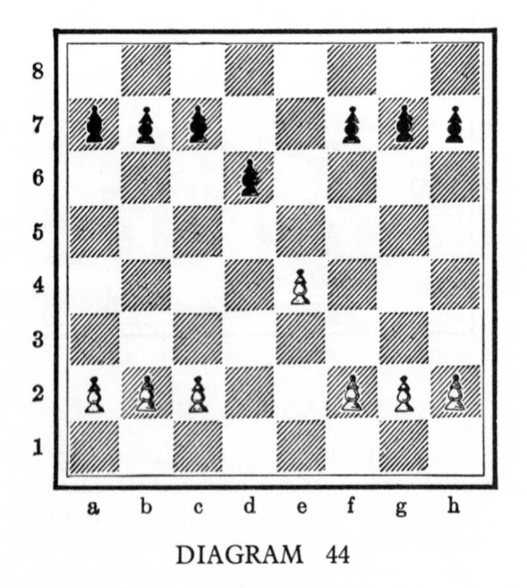

DIAGRAM 44

Black, in the meantime, will of course, also aim at the development of his Rooks. In the position of the Diagram it is even less troublesome for him than for White to prepare the opening of the d-file, as there is no objection to his playing immediately Kt-e7 with P-c6 and P-d5. The only reason which might deter Black from playing Kt-e7 is the fear that White might answer Bxf6 forcing Black to retake with the Pawn g7 and thereby tearing a hole in the protecting chain of Pawns around the King. However, as will be explained in the discussion of the middle game, this maneuver need not be feared.

The advance of the d-Pawn, besides the possibility of opening the d-file for the Rooks, has another very important purpose. It invites, and often compels the opponent to take the Pawn with his e-Pawn thereby losing control of "the center." What is meant by center in King's Pawn openings will be understood from the analysis of the Diagram 44 in which only the Pawn skeleton of a King's Pawn game is given and in which it is assumed that Black has exchanged the Pawn e5 for the Pawn d4. This Pawn formation offers an advantage to White because the Pawn e4, White's center-Pawn, controls the two squares d5 and f5 while the two corresponding squares in White's camp that is d4 and f4, are not in the hands of Black and could be occupied by White men. It is evident that it must be advantageous to have pieces placed in the center of the board as there they have naturally more mobility than towards the edge of the board where part of their radius of action is cut off. A Knight, for instance, placed on d4 will possibly have an opportunity later on to go to f5 from where he helps an attack on g7. The square f4 may be useful for the Queen in an attempt to reach the King's wing speedily, thus accumulating on that part of the board superior forces. These and other advantages connected with the control of the center will be more readily understood after the discussion of the middle game maneuvers of which the center squares form the basis. It is necessary, however, to touch upon this matter at this time, as in many openings the player is confronted after the very first moves with questions in which the maintenance of the center-Pawn is the point at issue.

Following are a few examples:

Supposing White, after (1) P-e4, P-e5, plays (2) P-d4. Then Black is immediately threatened with the loss of his center-Pawn, which he cannot defend with P-d6 as after (3) Pxe5, Pxe5 White would exchange Queens and thereby deprive Black of the possibility of bringing his Rooks quickly into coöperation through castling.

(2) . . ., Kt-c6 is out of question too; not on account of (3) P-d5, which merely helps Black in getting his Knight over to the King's wing via e7 and allows him to maintain his center-Pawn, but on account of (3) Pxe5, Ktxe5; (4) Pf4, which secures the control of the center for White and does not leave Black a chance to advance his Queen's Pawn to d5 with the view of depriving White of his center-Pawn too.

For these reasons Black has no choice but has to play (2) . . ., Pxd4. True enough, Black gives up his center-Pawn with this exchange, but White cannot prevent P-d5 in the long run, so that he also loses his center-Pawn and has no advantage over Black in that respect. The following variations are typical for the line of play in cases of this kind. White tries to hold back Black's Queen's Pawn as long as he can, but finally Black enforces the advance.

I.	(3) Qxd4	Kt-c6
	(4) Q-e3	

Now P-d5 is not possible because of Pxd5 check.

(4) . . .	Kt-f6
(5) Kt-c3	B-e7
(6) B-d2	P-d5

Threatening to win a piece by P-d4.

(7) Pxd5	Ktxd5

Now White has no center-Pawn either; Black has a perfectly good game.

II.	(3) Kt-f3	Kt-c6

Most players would be tempted to play P-c5 instead. But this must be bad as it is a Pawn move which is not necessary. Black does not need to defend the Pawn d4 as he is a Pawn ahead; and the development of the pieces is much more valuable than the advantage of a Pawn. White would obtain a far superior position with (4) P-c3, Pxc3; (5) Ktxc3, after which Black cannot hope ever to free his game by P-d5.

(4) Ktxd4	Kt-f6

It would be bad to exchange Knights on d4 because White's Queen would be brought up into a dominating position from which she could not easily be driven away.

(5) Kt-c3	B-b4

This attacks again the Pawn e4. Relieving the pin by (6) B-d2 would be no protection as Black could exchange on c3 and then take the Pawn. Therefore, White must defend the Pawn with another piece. The Bishop f1, which has to be developed in any case, offers himself naturally for this purpose, but B-d3 is not possible as long as the Knight d4 has to be kept protected by the Queen. Hence, it is necessary first to exchange the Knight.

(6) Ktxc6	Pb7xc6
(7) B-d3	P-d5 !

Again Black has succeeded in advancing his Queen's Pawn against the opposing center-Pawn, and White cannot avoid the exchange. To advance to e5 would be against the principle that no Pawn-move should be made in the opening which is not absolutely necessary. How easily (8) P-e5 could get White into trouble can be seen from the following variation: (8) . . ., Kt-g4; (9) o-o, o-o; (10) Pf4 ??, B-c5+; (11) K-h1, Q-h4; (12) P-h3, Q-g3; (13) Pxg4, Q-h4 mate.

III. (3) P-c3

With this move White invites Black to lose time in winning a Pawn or two while the White pieces are rapidly developed. If Black accepts the Gambit[1] the continuation might be.

(3) . . .	Pxc3
(4) B-c4	Pxb2
(5) Bxb2	

or

(4) . . .	Kt-c6
(5) Kt-f3	P-d6
(6) Ktxc3 or Q-b3 or o-o	

In all of these cases White has by far the freer game and he remains in the possession of his center-Pawn. For this reason it is much more advisable for Black to decline the Gambit offered and to hasten his development by immediately advancing his Queen's Pawn, thus:

(3) P-c3	P-d5 !
(4) Pxd5	

The advance of the King's Pawn would be quite out of place, as it would not add anything to White's development so that Black need not mind the loss of the move either which he sustains from the developing point of view in gaining a Pawn by Pxc3. The future development of Black is not any longer endangered as he has a Pawn in the center and an outlet for his Queen's Bishop.

[1] A Gambit is an opening in which the sacrifice of a Pawn is offered for the sake of a speedy development of the pieces.

(4) . . .	Qxd5
(5) Pxd4	Kt-c6
(6) Kt-f3	B-g4
(7) Kt-c3	Q-h5

and Black has, no doubt, the initiative.

If White, instead of playing (2) P-d4 as assumed in the above examples, advances his f-Pawn against Black's center, Black has ample time to make all preparations necessary to maintain his center-Pawn, for White does not threaten Pxe5 as long as he is not protected against Q-h4+, followed by Qxe4. Black's best move is apparently B-c5, so that he may be able to reply P-d6 to (3) Kt-f3 without blocking the way of the Bishop. On c5 Black's Bishop is very disagreeable for White as he prevents his castling. The natural development of this opening would be about this:

(2) P-f4	B-c5
(3) Kt-f3	P-d6
(4) B-c4	Kt-f6

Although this move blocks the diagonal for Black's Queen, making impossible a check on h4, it does not enable White to win a Pawn on e5, because (5) Pxe5, Pxe5; (6) Ktxe5 would be answered by Q-d4.

(5) P-d3	Kt-c6
(6) Kt-c3	B-g4

Black has one more piece developed than White on account of the Pawn move P-f4 which is a wasted move from the point of view of development, especially as White cannot very well castle on the King's side and make use of the open f-file for his Rooks.

The two principles mentioned—namely the development of the pieces without unnecessary Pawn moves or other loss of time and the maintenance of a Pawn in the center—are a perfectly sufficient guidance in all King's Pawn openings, as no particular difficulty exists for any piece to be developed to a favorable square. Even if Black tries to avoid the well-known openings which result from the reply (1) . . ., P-e5 by playing (1) . . ., P-e6 for instance, or (1) . . ., P-c5, or, in fact, any other of the twenty possible first moves, White will find the right way to mobilize his men if he strictly adheres to those two principles and resists the temptation to institute an early attack. A few examples will show how simple the application of the principle is.

I.	(1) P-e4	P-d5

This attacks White's Pawn and White has to decide whether to protect, advance or exchange him. The advance P-e5 and the protection P-f3 are out of question because these moves are Pawn moves which do not contribute to the development and are, therefore, to be classed as mere loss of time. The protection (2) P-d3 is not sufficient either as Black, after exchanging on e4, would hamper White's development by exchanging Queens so that White would lose the right of castling. The protection (2) Kt-c3 cannot be recommended as Black could deprive White of his center-Pawn and obtain one for himself by Pxe4, (3) Ktxe4; P-e5. For all these reasons White cannot do better than exchanges on d5.

At first sight this might seem a violation of the principles, as Pxd5 is a Pawn move which does not further the development of the pieces while Black, in retaking the Pawn, develops his Queen. However, as was already pointed out on several other occasions, the early development of the Queen is not desirable as she is sure to be exposed to the attack of minor pieces. Indeed, White obtains the better game through (3) Kt-c3, Q-a5; (4) P-d4 or (4) Kt-f3, followed by P-d4. Black cannot get his King's Pawn up to the center [(4) P-d4, P-e5; (5) Q-h5] and in addition he is bound to lose some more moves with his Queen as soon as White has developed his Bishop to d2 threatening a discovered attack through a move with the Knight c3.

II. (1) P-e4 P-e6

With this move Black switches the center from the e-file to the d-file.

(2) P-d4 P-d5

Now White need not hesitate to protect his King's Pawn with Kt-c3, for Black cannot as shown in example I gain control of the center by exchanging on e4 and playing P-e5.

The advance (3) P-e5 cannot be recommended for the reason explained in example I. Of course, White, being a move ahead anyhow, can afford to make a Pawn move which does not exactly advance his own development, if that Pawn move hampers the development of the opponent to some extent. This would be the case after (3) P-e5, as Black could not develop his King's Knight to the most natural square, namely, f6. However, the Pawns d4 and e5, though forming a strong center, as long as they are both in place, are liable to become subject to disagreeable attacks which Black can institute with P-c5 and P-f6, and if White cannot maintain his center, then the advance to e5 is mere waste of time.

(3) Kt-c3 Kt-f6

Again White's King's Pawn is attacked. The first continuation for White to think of would be (4) B-d3, developing another piece. However, Black can then simply exchange twice on e4 and play P-c5, so that White loses his Pawn center. P-e5 does not seem very good either. It does not lose any time, as Black too has to lose a move retreating with his Knight. But the latter is well posted on d7 from where he assists the contemplated advance P-c5 against White's center. The best continuation is apparently (4) B-g5, which develops a piece and protects the Pawn e4 through pinning the Knight f6. After

(4) B-g5 B-e7

White finally has to either advance the King's Pawn or exchange him. The latter seems preferable. The drawbacks to the advance have been discussed before. After the exchange White can develop his King's Bishop to d3 where he is considerably better posted than the corresponding Black Bishop.

QUEEN'S PAWN OPENINGS

The same two leading principles apply to Queen's Pawn openings which were discussed in connection with the King's Pawn openings; but there is one great difference between the two kinds of openings which is not obvious to the beginner. This is the fact that in Queen's Pawn openings, in most cases, neither player has a chance to open a file in the center of the board through the exchange of one of the center-Pawns, and that, therefore, an additional Pawn move is necessary in the opening stage to provide for an open file in which the Rooks later on may have an opportunity of entering the battle.

In addition, it is in most variations not easy to find a good place for the Queen's Bishop without further Pawn moves, and it is here where the beginner to bound to err in the plan of his mobilization unless he has adequate instruction.

In trying to open a file for the Rooks it will be advisable—just as in the King's Pawn openings—to aim at the same time at the clearing away of the opponent's center-Pawn, and this can only be done by the advance of the c-Pawn. Therefore, it would mean loss of time if the

Queen's Knight were developed into the c-file before the c-Pawn has moved; the Knight would have to be moved away again in order to enable the opening of the c-file. This consideration furnishes the key for the understanding of the most popular Queen's Pawn opening, which is

(1) P-d4	P-d5
(2) Kt-f3	Kt-f6
(3) P-c4	

White offers a Pawn to induce Black to give up his center-Pawn, hence the name "Queen's Gambit." If Black could actually hold the Pawn he would be justified in accepting the Gambit unless it can be demonstrated that White's advantage in development yields a winning attack. However, White can easily regain the Gambit-Pawn, and so there is absolutely no reason why Black should give up his Pawn-center.

The way in which White regains his Pawn in the accepted Gambit is this: (3) . . ., Pxc4; (4) P-e3, P-b5; (5) P-a4, P-c6 (if Black takes the Pawn a4, White captures the Pawn c4 and then regains the a-Pawn. (5) . . ., P-a6, cannot be played on account of Pxb5, opening the a-file for White's Rook so that Black cannot retake the Pawn). (6) P-b3, Pxb3; (7) Pxb5, Pxb5; (8) Bxb5+ and Qxb3.

Now White is far ahead in the development and in addition he has an open file for his Queen's Rook in which the black Pawn is bound to be lost in the long run. Moreover, Black has no compensation for White's strong Pawn-center.

For this reason the Queen's Gambit is hardly ever accepted and the following defense played instead:

(1) P-d4	P-d5
(2) Kt-f3	Kt-f6
(3) P-c4	P-e6
(4) Kt-c3	

Black has now the choice between either advancing his c-Pawn right away or first developing the pieces of his Queen's wing. In the latter case he cannot place the Queen's Knight on c6 as this would block the way of the c-Pawn. He must develop him to d7. This appears to be a bad move as it blocks the way of the Queen's Bishop, but this Bishop will have to be developed in a different diagonal anyway as the Pawn e6 cannot advance opening the diagonal c8-h3.

I.	(4) . . .	Ktb8-d7
	(5) B-g5	

The fact that White can develop his Queen's Bishop without difficulty while Black cannot do so has made the Queen's Gambit one of the most popular openings.

(5) . . .	B-e7
(6) P-e3	o-o
(7) B-d3	P-b6
(8) o-o	B-b7
(9) Pxd5	Pxd5
(10) R-c1	

White is two moves ahead in the development, as Black has still to move his c-Pawn before he can get his Queen's Rook into play. In the meantime White can mobilize his King's Rook with Q-e2 and Rf1-d1, with a view to opening the Queen's file by Pd4xc5.

II. (4) . . . P-c5

If White now Plays P-e3, holding his Pawn-center, a symmetrical development follows on both sides. If, however, White takes his opportunity to develop the Queen's Bishop, a game of entirely different character ensues. The following variations show typical examples of the way these two variations are liable to develop:

A.	(5) P-e3	Kt-c6
	(6) P-a3	

If White played (6) P-b3 before castling he would get into trouble because Black could pin his Queen's Knight with Pxd4 and B-b4. For this reason the maneuver P-a3, Pxc5, P-b4 and B-b2 is usually adopted to develop the Queen's Bishop. It is true that this maneuver involves two Pawn moves, which mean a loss of time, instead of only one, as for instance when playing (6) B-d3, (7) o-o, (8) P-b3, (9) B-b2. But Black can hardly avoid a similar loss of time. For if he plays (6) . . ., B-d6, he loses two moves with his Bishop through recapturing on c5 (after (7) Pxc5) and going back to d6; and if he first exchanges on d4 and then develops the Bishop to d6, White has an open diagonal for his Queen's Bishop and need not make any more Pawn moves to develop him while Black still must move his Queen's Knight's Pawn to get his Queen's Bishop into play.

(6) . . .	P-a6
(7) Pxc5	Bxc5
(8) P-b4	B-d6

(9)	B-b2	Pxc4
(10)	Bxc4	P-b5
(11)	B-d3	B-b7

B. (5) Pxd5 Pxd5

The idea of this exchange is to create a weak Pawn on d5 against which later on an attack can be instituted. However, it is very doubtful whether the Pawn on d5 is really weak. Experience has shown that Black wins just as many games as White in this opening; the reason is probably that White, in order to open the Queen's file for attack on d5, has to give away his center-Pawn so that Black has more freedom for his pieces in the center.

(6)	P-g3	Kt-c6
(7)	B-g2	B-e6
(8)	B-g5	B-e7
(9)	o-o	o-o
(10)	Pxc5	Bxc5
(11)	R-c1	B-e7

(12) Kt-d4 or Q-a4
followed by Rf1-d1.

Instead of developing the King's Bishop to g2 White can just as well play (6) B-g5 or f4, (7) P-e3 and (8) B-d3. In either case the success depends rather on clever maneuvering in the middle-game than on an advantage inherent to the opening.

What has been said of irregular replies which Black may try in King's Pawn openings holds good in Queen's Pawn openings too. There is no series of opening moves which needs to be memorized. The principles of speedy development and of the maintenance of a Pawn center lead the right way in all novel openings which a player might try to avoid the well-known paths which have been studied out by the masters of many generations.

Following are again a few examples which show the application of the principles:

I. (1) P-d4 P-c5
(2) P-e3

With Pxc5 White would give away his center-Pawn, and Black would regain the Gambit-Pawn easily after (2) . . ., P-e6. White could play (2) P-d5, thereby depriving Black's Queen's Knight of his best developing square. But in doing so he would lose time with a Pawn move which does not improve the mobility of his own pieces, and consequently (2) P-e3 is preferable.

II.	(1) P-d4	Kt-f6
	(2) Kt-f3	

The advance P-c4 which, as explained, is customary in Queen's Pawn openings, serves its original purpose only if Black has a Pawn on d5 so that White can open the c-file. Therefore, it is better for White to wait until Black shows what intentions he has with his Queen's Pawn.

(2) . . .	P-d6
(3) Kt-c3	

Black's last move clearly indicates that he intends playing P-e5 and not P-d5, and so White has no reason to expect that he will be able to open the c-file for his Rooks. Consequently there is no objection to his developing the Queen's Knight to c3, blocking the c-Pawn.

(3) . . .	Ktb8-d7
(4) B-f4	

This prevents P-e5 for the time being, and Black has to make rather complicated preparations, such as P-c6 and Q-c7 before he can advance the King's Pawn two squares. In other words, White completes his development more quickly than Black and he has consequently the better winning chances, provided, of course, he knows how to maintain his advantage in the middle game and in the end game.

THE MIDDLE GAME

It is not possible to draw a distinct dividing line between the two stages of the game which are called the *Opening* and the *Middle game.* Strictly speaking the opening comprises only such moves as are *necessary* for the development of the pieces, and any move which a player—without being compelled—makes with a piece that is already developed, ought to be regarded as a Middle-game move. To give an example: If after (1) P-e4, P-e5; (2) Kt-f3, Kt-c6; (3) Kt-c3, Kt-f6; (4) B-b5 Black plays Kt-d4, he deviates from the Opening and embarks on a Middle-game maneuver; for the Queen's Knight was already developed.

This does not mean that it is bad under all circumstances to make a Middle-game move during the opening stage of a game. But only such moves should be considered in cases of this kind as a player is fairly sure to make at any rate within the further course of the game with a view to increasing the mobility of the piece in question.

This is the main point. A second move made with a piece must improve its position, otherwise, common sense tells us, it is surely bad. For instance: After (1) P-e4, P-e5; (2) Kt-f3, Kt-c6; (3) B-b5, Kt-f6; (4) o-o, B-e7 there is no objection to White's playing (5) R-e1 as the Rook will very likely want to get into action in the e-file in any case, as soon as the development has progressed with P-d4, Kt-c3, B-g5, etc.

But if in an opening like (1) P-e4, P-e5; (2) Kt-f3, Kt-c6; (3) B-c4, Kt-f6 White plays (4) Kt-g5 for instance, or (4) B-d5, it is evident that he merely wastes time, for in the first case he places the Knight on a square from which he is sure to be driven away again as soon as the direct attack involved in his move has been warded off, and in the second case he moves the Bishop to a square which does not afford him any more mobility than the one on which he stood before.

As a rule only Rooks or Knights are in a position, during the opening, to add to their mobility by a second move; the Rooks by occupying a file which is liable to be opened by an exchange of Pawns, and the Knights by occupying a square in the center of the board.

The Knights are really more often under the necessity of making several moves in succession than any other piece, because they can never pass over more than one line at a time, and they may be required to hasten from one wing of the board to the other just as often as the other pieces. This is the reason why the most favorable spot for a Knight is a square in the center of the board; there he is always ready for an excursion to either wing.

The establishment of a Knight in the center can more readily be effected in Queen's Pawn openings than in King's Pawn openings. This will be evident from the following consideration:

In Queen's Pawn openings the squares e5 and e4 are the ones which are aimed at by the respective Knights. If the opponent exchanges the Knight with either his Queen's Knight or his King's Bishop, the Pawn which takes the place of the Knight in recapturing, gains control of two squares in the heart of the hostile camp. To illustrate this by a case which often occurs: If after (1) P-d4, P-d5; (2) Kt-f3, Kt-f6; (3) P-e3, P-c5; (4) B-d3, Kt-c6; (5) o-o, P-e6; (6) P-b3, B-d6; (7) B-b2, o-o; (8) Ktb1-d2, P-b6; (9) Kt-e5 Black plays Bxe5, White in retaking drives Black's King's Knight away depriving the King's wing of an important protection and also creating a weakness on d6, where White might be able at some later stage of the game to establish his Knight. Another advantage of the position for White is that he can get his King's Rook into play by P-f4 and R-f3-h3, while Black's Rook cannot get to f6 as long as White has his Pawn on e5.

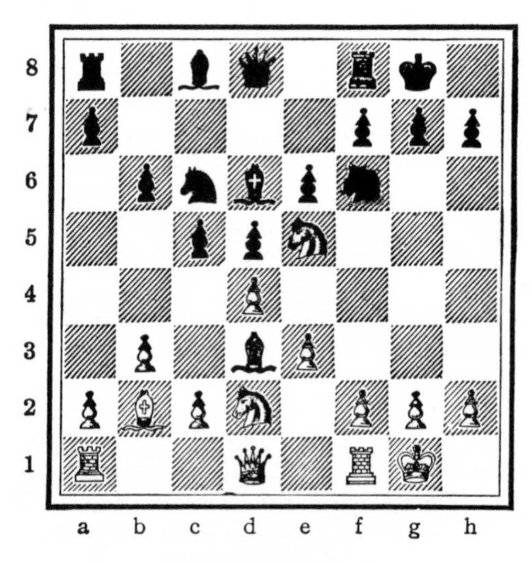

DIAGRAM 45

In King's Pawn openings the situation is different. Here the squares d5 and d4 respectively are the aim of the Knights which normally are posted on c3 and c6. However, as long as the opposing King's Knight can exchange himself for the advancing Queen's Knight there is no advantage in occupying the center. The position of Diagram 46 is a typical example. If White plays Kt-d5 he loses practically a move, as after Ktxd5, Pxd5 he has in no way improved the mobility of his men while it is Black's turn to move. In addition, White, by transferring his Pawn to d5, gives up his Pawn-center and blocks a diagonal which his Bishop could use, while Black, in retreating with his Knight to e7, gains a move towards the efficient use of the Knight on the King's wing.

All the same, the advance of the Queen's Knight in the center is one of the most important maneuvers in King's Pawn openings when it is properly prepared, and its consequences need thorough discussion.

The proper preparation consists in first fixing the object at which the Knight aims. This— from White's, the attacker's point of view—is the

Knight f6. The developing move B-g5 serves this purpose in the most natural way, and a position arises similar to the one shown in Diagram 43 where Black prevented any further accumulation of white forces on f6 by B-e6. In the present case this move is of doubtful value as White, by P-d4, can force Black to give up his center-Pawn.

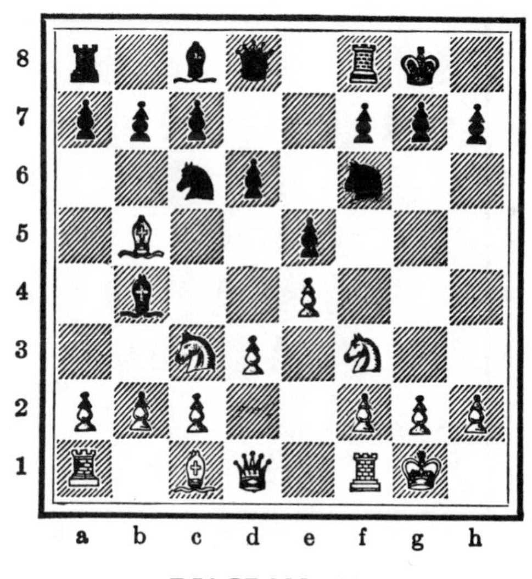

DIAGRAM 46

If Black is ready to admit that Kt-d5 is a disagreeable threat he will either exchange the Knight for his Bishop b4 or he will play Kt-e7 in order to take White's Knight should he go to d5. Ordinarily Black plays first Bxc3 and then Kt-e7. The reason is that this maneuver enables Black to get his Queen's Knight over to the King's wing while White's Bishop b5 is rather out of action, so that Black has a good chance to enter the battle on the King's wing with one piece more than White. Of course, White can get his Bishop into play again by placing him on c4. But he has to spend a move in doing so, which does not add to the completion of the development.

In the position of Diagram 46 Black would not take any steps to prevent Kt-d5 unless a threat is involved in this move which cannot be counteracted by the most natural continuation, which is the development of the Bishop c8. Indeed, there seems to be no reason why Black should not answer (1) B-g5 with B-g4 and (2) Kt-d5 with Kt-d4; for the Knight f6, who after Kt-d5 is attacked twice, is defended twice, and there is no possibility for White to attack the Knight again. On the other hand, the attack on the Bishop b4 is balanced by the attack on the Bishop b5, and if White were to withdraw his Bishop to c4 Black could withdraw his to c5.

However, in the position resulting after these moves (Diagram 47)

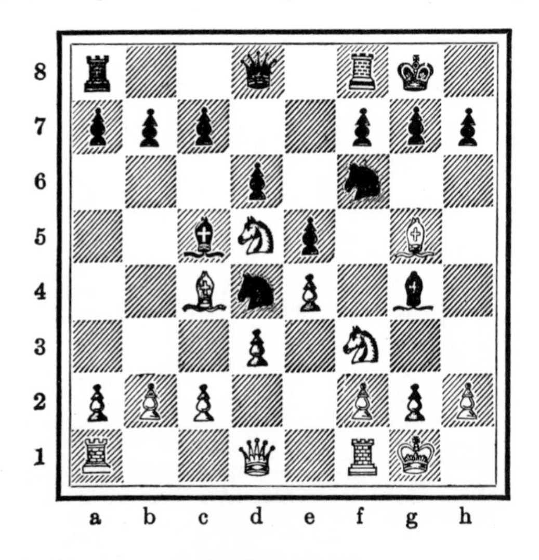

DIAGRAM 47

White gets the upper hand because he is one move ahead in the attack on the opposing King's Knight. The danger of the concentration of two pieces on this Knight lies in the fact that Black is obliged to retake with the g-Pawn in case White exchanges on f6 and that thereby the squares f6 and h6 lose their natural protection. Thus weak points are created of which White may find an opportunity to make use in a manner similar to the one illustrated by the discussion of Diagrams 26 and 29. On the other hand, Black gains an open file for his Rooks as soon as the g-Pawn is out of the way, and the exchange on f6 should therefore not be made until preparations for the occupation of the resulting weak spots are completed. The following variations will throw some light on this rather complex problem.

Supposing White wants to try the immediate exchange on f6, hoping that somehow or other he will be able to take advantage of the weakness resulting on f6 and h6. In exchanging he can give up either his Knight d5 or his Bishop g5. In both cases there are promising possibilities for attack, but Black, with correct play, can sufficiently defend himself and even get the better.

If White plays (1) Ktxf6 he has to lose a move before he can bring up other pieces to help in the attack, for after Pxf6 he must first move the Bishop g5. The only good square for the Bishop is h4 from where he maintains the pin on f6 which would become very dangerous for Black if he could not prevent White's Queen from entering on h6 or render the double threat on f6 ineffective in some other way. The logical continuation for Black is to answer (2) B-h4 with K-h8 in order to occupy the g-file with his Rook as soon as possible. Indeed, this is at the same time the best defense against White's threat, for if White now plays (3) Q-d2, Black replies Ktxf3+; (4) Pxf3, Bxf3; and he is the first to take advantage of the open g-file as his King has already made room for the Rook.

It would be dangerous for Black to play (3) . . ., Bxf3 instead of Ktxf3. For White would continue (4) Q-h6 and the only way for Black to prevent the disaster threatened on f6 is to give back the piece he just won: (4) . . ., Kt-e2+; (5) K-h1, Bxg2+; (6) Kxg2, R4-g8+; (7) K-h1, R-g6; or (6) . . ., Kt-f4+; (7) K-h1, Kt-g6. In either case Black's defense is very difficult.

The play outlined in the last variation suggests a better method for White to institute the attack in the position of Diagram 47. This is the preparatory move (1) Q-d2. (1) Bxf6 is obviously not as good, as Black can soon drive away the Knight d5 by P-c6, relieving f6 of all pressure.

In answer to (1) Q-d2, which threatens (2) Bxf6, (3) Q-h6, (4) Ktxf6 and (5) Qxh7 mate, Black has three replies, namely: Bxf3 or Ktxf3 or P-c6.

That (1) . . ., Bxf3 is not sufficient can easily be seen. White continues (2) Bxf6, Q-d7; (3) Kt-e7±, and Black must give up the Queen for the Knight as (3) . . ., K-h8 would be followed by (4) Bxg7+, (5) Q-g5+ and (6) Q-f6 mate. It is interesting to note that it is just the one move which White is ahead in the development that gives him the win. If he tried to checkmate Black by (3) Q-g5, P-g6; (4) Q-h6 he would be checkmated himself by (4) . . ., Kt-e2+ followed by Bxg2+ and Q-g4+, etc.

(2) . . ., Pxf6 would not be of avail either. The consequence would be: (3) Q-h6, Kt-e2+; (4) K-h1, Bxg2+; (5) Kxg2, Kt-f4+; (6) Ktxf4, Pxf4; (7) K-h1, K-h8; (8) R-g1, R-g8; (9) Rxg8+, Qxg8; (10) R-g1 and the mate can only be averted by the sacrifice of the Queen for the Rook.

The second defense which Black could try is (1) . . ., Ktxf3+; (2) Pxf3, Bxf3. Now (3) Bxf6, Pxf6; (4) Q-h6 would be fatal for White as Black plays K-h8 and there is no protection against the threat R-g8+. But White can again make a preparatory move which secures for him the victory. This is (3) P-h3, with the view to make room for the Rook by K-h2. The only way to counter White's threat is now P-c6. However, after (4) Ktxf6+, Pxf6; (5) B-h4, K-h8; (6) K-h2, R-g8; (7) R-g1, Q-e7; (8) R-g3 Black is unable to stave off defeat any longer. Whatever he plays, White succeeds in attacking f6 for the second time while Black has no second protection at his disposal. For instance, (8) . . ., B-h5; (9) Q-h6, B-g6; (10) R-f3—or (8) . . ., Rxg3; (9) Pxg3 and (10) Rf1.

The most interesting line of defense is the third one mentioned, that is (1) . . ., P-c6. After (2) Ktxf6+, Pxf6; (3) B-h4 a situation arises similar to the one discussed in the line of play commencing with (1) Ktxf6+, but with the big difference that White is now one move ahead in the attack. This is the move Q-d2 in answer to which Black was forced to make the move P-c6 which does not improve the constellation of the Black pieces in any way.

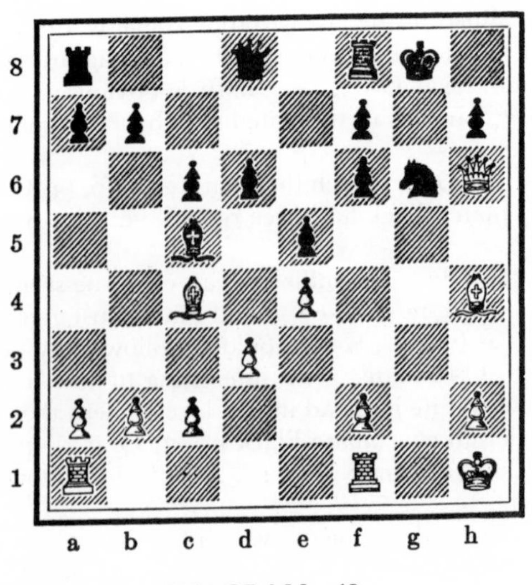

DIAGRAM 48

This one move is sufficient to secure for White an easy victory. After (3) . . ., Bxf3; (4) Q-h6, Kt-e2+; (5) K-h1, Bxg2+; (6) Kxg2,

Kt-f4+; (7) K-h1, Kt-g6 the position of Diagram 48 is reached in which White can force the mate, or win Black's Queen in a most ingenious manner. If White tried to win by (8) R-g1, threatening mate in four moves through Rxg6, Qxg6, Q-h6 and R-g1 Black could sufficiently defend himself with (8) . . ., P-d5, unpinning the Pawn f7 and enabling B-e7, which would supply the much needed protection for the square f6. However, White can frustrate Black's intention by playing (8) P-d4 !! If Black takes with the Pawn, (9) P-e5 follows forcing Pd6xe5 after which Black cannot any more intercept the diagonal of the Bishop c4 so that there remains no defense against (10) R-g1. If, on the other hand, Black takes the Pawn d4 with his Bishop, White continues with (9) P-c3, B-c5; (10) Ra1-d1, again preventing the interception of the Bishop c4 and threatening R-g1. The consequence could then be: (10) . . ., K-h8; (11) R-g1, Q-e7; (12) R-d3, R-g8; (13) R-h3, Ktxh4; (14) Qxh7+ and (15) Rxh4 mate, or: (13) . . ., R-g7; (14) R-f3, Ra8-g8; (15) Bxf6, Q-d7; (16) R-h3 and the mate on h7 can only be avoided by the sacrifice of the Queen for the Rook.

The foregoing variations show conclusively that the position of Diagram 47 is lost for Black. The attack which White obtains after creating a weakness on f6 by the removal of the Pawn g7 cannot be effectively countered. The question arises, whether Black was at fault when disregarding White's threat to place his Knight on d5 and developing his Queen's Bishop or whether he had a chance to improve on one of the two following moves which led to the position of Diagram 47. Indeed, it lies near to try the same attack which White threatens to initiate by Q-d2 one move earlier by playing Q-d7 instead of B-c5. The fact, however, that this Bishop is not coöperating with the pieces on the King's wing makes a big difference and the most Black can obtain is apparently a draw. The continuation could be: (1) Ktxf6+, Pxf6; (2) Bxf6, P-h6; (3) P-c3, Ktxf3+, (4) Pxf3, B-h5; (5) K-h1, K-h7; (6) R-g1, R-g8; (7) R-g3. If Black's Bishop were on c5 instead of b4, White could not play R-g3 on account of Bxf2. He would have to make the preparatory move Q-e2 and he would be lost after R-g6, just in the same manner which was demonstrated in one of the above variations with attack and defense reversed. As it is Black cannot enter on h3 with his Queen without exchanging Rooks and so he is unable to take advantage of the weakness on f3. After (7) . . ., R-g6, (8) B-h4, B-a5 or c5, (9) P-d4 and Q-d3 the game probably ends in a draw as it is unlikely that White can realize an advantage from the doubled Pawn which he is ahead.

To the beginner the lines of play discussed in connection with

Diagrams 47 and 48 will have appeared rather complicated. This they are, indeed, even for the experienced player; but it is by no means necessary to memorize any of the variations. The important thing to realize is the fact that in a position where both players have castled on the King's side, a dangerous weakness is created if the g-Pawn is forced

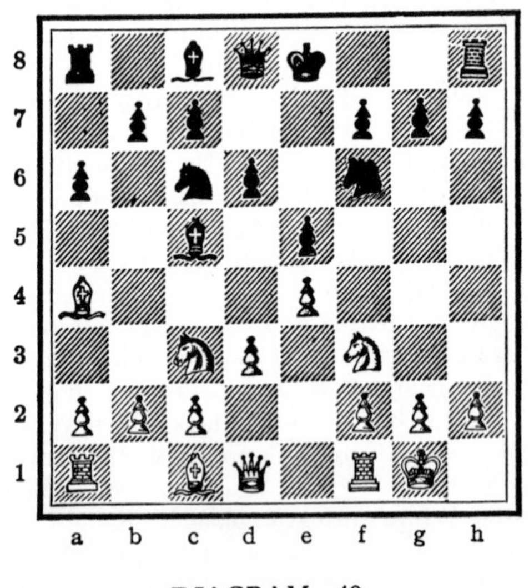

DIAGRAM 49

to move, and if pressure can be brought to bear upon the two squares which through the move of the g-Pawn have lost their protection; moreover, that a method to create such a weakness is the pinning of the hostile King's Knight and the advance of the Queen's Knight in the center.

Another important point that the variations discussed will bring out to the observant reader is the order in which the different pieces take their turn in the battle. First come the minor pieces, then the Queen and then the Rooks. This, of course, is not a rule that has to be adhered to under all circumstances, but in most games it is a good rule to follow. The reason is obvious. The Rooks have no opportunity of making themselves useful until a file has been opened, while the Queen often finds an occasion to enter the battlefield on a diagonal. Sometimes a Rook, rather than getting into play via one of the center-files, finds an attacking opportunity on the wing, after the Pawn in front of the Rook has advanced. Usually this is feasible only in games in which the players have not castled on the same side of the board.

The following example, taken from an actual game, furnishes a good illustration. After White's seventh move the position of Diagram 49 was reached, in which Black continued with P-b5 with the view to playing B-g4 and Kt-d4. White replied (8) B-b3, B-g4; (9) Kt-e2. Better would surely have been B-e3, which develops a new piece. To allow the exchange of f3 which forces the g-Pawn out is dangerous because Black may castle on the Queen's side and storm with the Pawns of his King's wing. From Black's next move, Q-d7, it is indeed apparent that he has decided on a maneuver of this kind. The game continued: (10) P-c3, Bxf3; (11) Pxf3, Q-h3; (12) Kt-g3, P-h5; (13) B-e3. He cannot play R-e1 on account of Bxf2+ followed by Qxh2+ and Qxg3. (13) . . ., P-h4; (14) Kt-h1, R-h6 and wins, for if White takes the Rook, Pxh6 opens the g-file and the other Rook occupies it with deadly effect.

In the last example it was easy for the Rooks to take an active part in the battle because a file was open which enabled them to bear down on the opposing King. In the majority of cases no open file is available on the wing and the attack with the Rooks is then much more difficult. There is little use in advancing the Pawns on the wing on which the hostile King has castled unless one of them can be exchanged so that a line is opened which the Rooks can occupy. As a rule such an exchange is only possible in case one of the Pawns in front of the King has moved. In the position of Diagram 50 for instance, White is able to open the h-file by advancing the h-Pawn and exchanging it against Black's g-Pawn, while Black, who would like to use his Rooks in an attack on the Queen's wing, has little hope to open a file on that side of the board. If Black's g-Pawn were still on his original square, the advance of White's h-Pawn would be of no avail. Black would simply wait until the Pawn has advanced to h6 and then he would play P-g6 so that White's own Pawn would block the h-file for the Rook. In the above position, which occurred in one of six simultaneous games played by the author in a blindfold-exhibition, the attack developed as follows:

(1) P-h4	P-b5
(2) B-b3	Kt-a5
(3) P-h5	Ktxb3
(4) Pa2xb3	Q-a5

Black has succeeded in opening a line also, but he cannot get his Rooks working in it. His last move threatens mate in two moves by

Q-a1; Kt-b1, Bxb2; but White simply defends himself first against this threat and then proceeds with his attack on the King's wing which is irresistible.

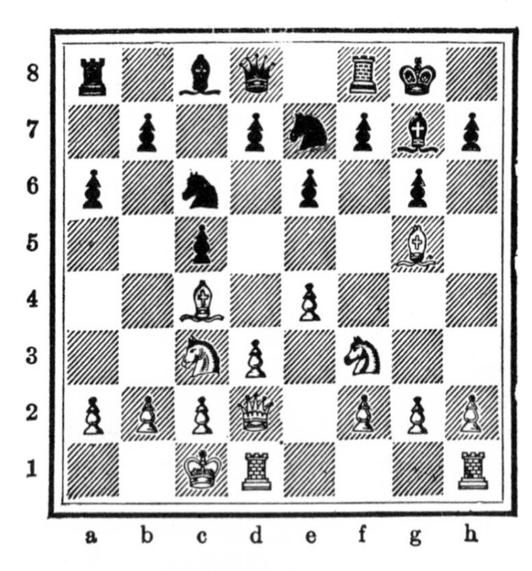

DIAGRAM 50

(5) K-b1	Kt-c6
(6) Pxg6	Pf7xg6
(7) B-h6	R-f7
(8) Bxg7	Rxg7

With this exchange White has weakened the defense around Black's King who has now only the Rook and himself to rely on for protection.

(9) Kt-g5	P-d5

Black opens the seventh rank in the hope that it will enable his Queen's Rook or his Queen to come to assistance. But so great is the advantage afforded White by the open h-file that he can sacrifice his Knight to break through Black's chain of defense and force the mate before Black has a chance to touch his Queen or his Rook.

(10) Ktxh7	Rxh7

If Q-c7 or Ra8-a7, White continues (11) Q-h6 ! Rxh7 ?; (12) Qxg6+, K-h8; (13) Q-e8+, K-g7; (14) Rxh7+, Kxh7; (15) R-h1+, etc.

(11)	Rxh7	Kxh7
(12)	R-h1+	K-g7
(13)	Q-h6+	K-f7
(14)	Q-h7+	K-f6
(15)	Q-h8+	K-e7
(16)	R-h7+	K-d6
(17)	Q-f8+	K-e5
(18)	P-f4+	K-d4
(19)	Q-f6+	K-e3
(20)	R-h3+	K-d2
(21)	Q-h4	

and Black resigns as there is no defense against Q-f2.

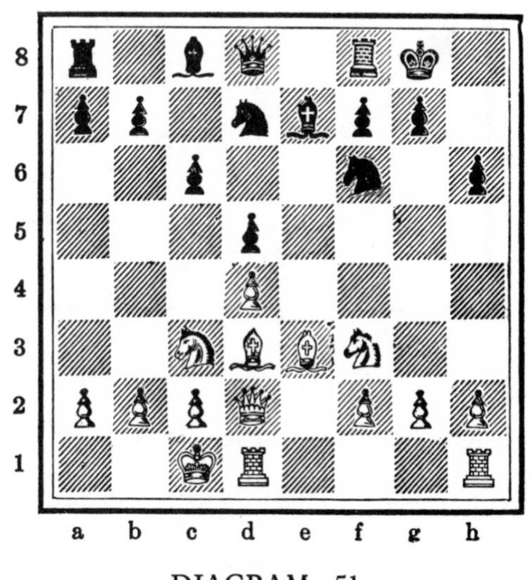

DIAGRAM 51

Diagram 51 shows a similar example, the only difference being that it is not the advance of the Black Knight's Pawn but that of the Rook's Pawn which gives White an opportunity of opening a file for his Rooks. He will accomplish this by advancing his Knight's Pawn to g5 and exchanging him against Black's Rook's Pawn. If he does not want to play P-g4 on the first move, because Black could take the Pawn with his Knight, he can prepare the advance by R-g1. But he need not really fear the loss of the Pawn, because in taking him Black would himself open the g-file for White's Rook and White is sure to obtain an overwhelming attack. It would, of course, be futile for Black to try and stop the advance of White's g-Pawn by P-g5, as White would then simply open the Rook's file by P-h4 and Pxg5, quite apart from the fact that he could sacrifice his Bishop e3 for two Pawns, thereby depriving Black's King of all protection. The play might proceed like this: (1) P-g4, P-g5; (2) Bxg5, Pxg5; (3) Qxg5+, K-h8; (4) Q-h6+,

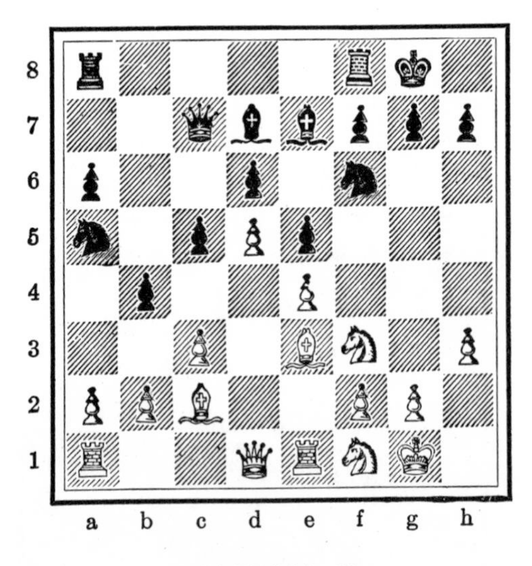

DIAGRAM 52

K-g8; (5) P-g5, Kt-e4; (6) Ktxe4, Pxe4; (7) P-g6, Pxg6; (8) Qxg6+, K-h8; (9) R-g1, etc.

Ordinarily both players castle on the same side of the board so that neither of them can advance his Pawns in an attack against the opposing King without weakening his own King's position. Only if a player holds more territory and has a greater number of pieces on the King's wing than the opponent he can embark on an attack which involves an advance of the Pawns in front of his King. Diagram 52 offers a typical example. Black has a preponderance on the Queen's side, while White has more mobility for his pieces on the King's side. Considering that Black cannot easily throw his men over to the King's wing, White can risk to loosen his Pawns on this wing without fearing that Black will be able to obtain a foothold on the weak points which are necessarily created by the advance of the Pawns in White's camp.

White will start the attack with (1) P-g4 and (2) Kt-g3. Then he threatens to occupy the dominating square f5 with his Knight, and Black has hardly any other move than P-g6; for if he permits Kt-f5 with the view to exchanging the Knight with his Bishop, he opens the g-file for White's Rooks. P-g6 on the other hand enables White to open the h-file by advancing the h-Pawn after the necessary preparations such as K-g2, R-h1, P-g5, etc.

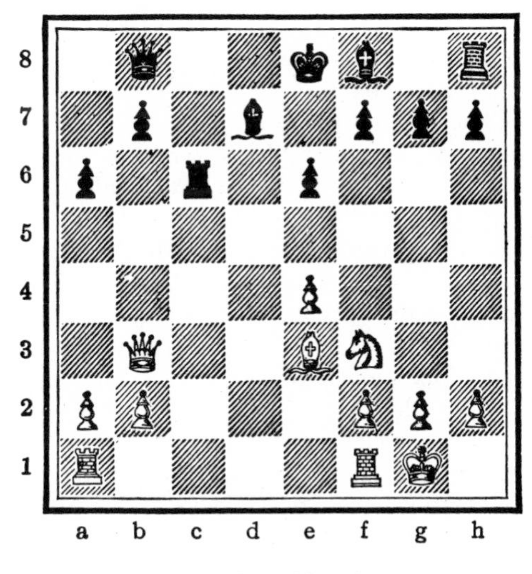

DIAGRAM 53

In the vast majority of games files for the Rooks are not opened on the side but in the center of the board, as was explained in the discussion of the openings. The many advantages arising from the control of a center-file by the Rooks will be more fully analyzed in the illustrative games. Generally speaking it is easier to get the two Rooks into coöperation in the center than on the side of the board. This coöperation—usually effected by doubling in one file—is naturally very important and it is the main reason why it is desirable to castle as early as possible. Between the Rooks of a player who is prevented from castling there are, so to speak, no natural lines of communication and it takes so long to create artificial ones that in most cases the opponent can, in the meantime, force a victory through the combined efforts of his Rooks. Diagram 53 gives an example. It is White's move, and he will naturally think of a Rook's move as all the other pieces are already developed. The best move is probably (1) Rf1-d1. Ra1-d1 comes also into consideration but this Rook might be needed later on the c-file while the King's Rook certainly will have no chance to be developed in any but the d-file as long as the White e- and f-Pawns are still on the board. Black, in the game from which the above position is taken, replied B-c5, and White continued with (2) Q-c3, attacking the Bishop c5 and the Pawn g7 at the same time.

Black has only the choice between returning with the Bishop to f8 or capturing on e3. Naturally, he chooses the latter move as he cannot improve his position by a retrogressive play which still further retards his development. After Bxe3, (3) Qxg7, Bxf2+; (4) Kxf2 R-c2+; (5) K-g1, R-f8; there is not much hope for Black to bring his King's Rook in contact with the other pieces, while White may be able to double his Rooks in the Queen's file, which would decide the victory as Black has no possibility to counter the threat R-d8+ in the long run. White played (6) Kt-e5 with the intention to sacrifice the Knight on f7 in case Black should move his Bishop. Rxf7 would then be followed by Q-g8+ and Qxb8 or Qxe6 mate. Therefore, Black has to withdraw his Rook with (6) . . ., R-c7 and White simply played (7) R-d2 threatening to double. Black prevented this by B-a4, at the same time threatening P-f6, but after (8) Kt-g4, R-c2; (9) R-d4, Q-c8; (10) Kt-f6+, K-e7; (11) Q-g5 he resigned as now the square c1 is sufficiently protected while the threat Kt-g8++ cannot be parried.

The foregoing examples show that generally several moves are necessary in the middle game for Knights and Rooks to reach positions favorable for an active part in the attack. With the Bishops it is different. They can usually be developed on their first move to the square on which they are needed in the middle game for either attack or defense.

In King's Pawn openings as well as in Queen's Pawn openings White's Queen's Bishop is, in the majority of cases, used for pinning Black's King's Knight on g5 and Black's King's Bishop is placed on e7 to relieve the pin. The pinning of the King's Knight, however, is not advisable in positions in which the opponent has the option of castling to the Queen's side. After (1) P-e4, P-e5; (2) Kt-f3, Kt-c6; (3) B-c4, Kt-f6; (4) Kt-c3, B-c5; (5) P-d3, P-d6; for instance White should wait with B-g5 until Black has castled on the King's side. If he plays (6) B-g5, Black will answer B-e6; (7) o-o, Q-d7; and now White would only hurt his own game by exchanging on f6 as the open g-file is bound to aid Black, who will castle on the Queen's side, in an attack on the King's side.

In Queen's Pawn openings the move B-g5 is always good as Black cannot very well castle on the Queen's side on account of the open c-file in which White would soon obtain an overwhelming attack. Another good square for the Queen's Bishop is in Queen's Pawn openings b2 from where the Bishop supports the advance of the King's Knight to e5. In this case the Queen's Knight should be developed to d2 instead of c3 so as not to obstruct the line of the Bishop. The same holds good for the development of Black's Queen's Bishop.

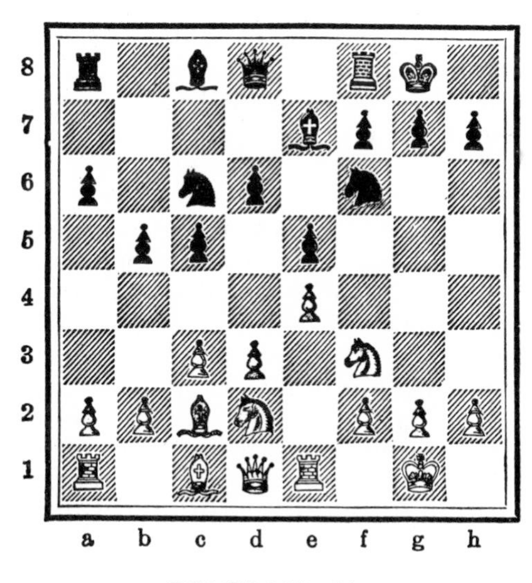

DIAGRAM 54

In King's Pawn openings it is dangerous for the Queen's Bishop to leave the long diagonal in which he is originally posted as the opponent might threaten to gain a foothold in the f-line with a Knight, provoking a weakening move with the g-Pawn. The position of Diagram 54, which occurred in a game between Teichmann and Rubinstein in the Karlsbad Tournament, 1911, furnishes an instructive example. White played (1) P-a4, trying to make use of the advanced position of Black's b-Pawn for opening the a-file for his Rook, and Black replied B-b7. This crosses White's plan, as after (2) Pxb5, Pxb5; it would not be White but Black who would gain control of the a-line. However, Black should not have withdrawn the Bishop from the King's wing, for White can now play his Queen's Knight via f1 and g3 or e3 to f5 unless Black weakens his Pawn position by P-g6. The proper way to answer White's first move would have been either B-e6 or P-b4. The latter is a Pawn move, but in the present case it cannot be considered a loss of time as White, too, has made a Pawn move which does not further his development.

The game went on as follows: (2) Kt-f1, Q-c7; (3) Kt-g3, P-g6; White's aim is accomplished. He has provoked a weakness which furnishes a mark for his attack. The way to conduct the attack—after completing the development by B-g5, will be to open the f-file for the Rook by advancing the f-Pawn. This advance can be prepared by P-h3 and Kt-h2. Of course, White would prefer to do without the move of the h-Pawn; but h2 is the only favorable square for the Knight f3, as neither from d2 nor from h4 has he an opportunity to help the attack while from h2 he may go to g4, bearing on both of the weak squares f6 and h6.

Black has little chance for counterattack. The only thing he can do is occupy the Queen's file with his Rooks and opening it by P-d5 and Pxe4. His Queen's Bishop, however, is badly placed in any case as he has no open diagonal to work in, and he will have to get back into play via his original square c8.

White's King's Bishop is not well placed either and is practically condemned to play the rôle of a Pawn by protecting the square d3 without, at the same time, attacking anything. There is, of course, a chance for him to be useful in the diagonal a2-g8. It may be said that in King's Pawn openings White's King's Bishop comparatively seldom has an opportunity to take an active part in the battle. He is mostly exchanged at an early stage of the game for Black's Queen's Knight or Queen's Bishop. In Queen's Pawn openings, however, he finds a great field of action in the unobstructed diagonal b1-h7. In this diagonal he can also be used in all openings starting with P-e4 in which Black does not advance his King's pawn to e5, as White can open the diagonal at any time by playing P-e5.

Generally speaking, Bishops should not be placed in diagonals which are obstructed by Pawns of their own army, and Pawns moves should be avoided which close a diagonal formerly open to a kindred Bishop. A striking illustration of the importance of this rule will be found in the play which developed in the position of Diagram 55 in a game between Teichmann and Dus Chotimirski in the Prague Tournament 1908. Black, on the move, played (1) . . ., Kt-e5, disturbing the symmetry of the position to his advantage by opening the diagonal of his Queen's Bishop without allowing White to make a similar maneuver. After (2) Ktxe5, Bxe5; (3) Q-e2, 0-0; (4) Ra1-d1, Q-e7; White yielded the temptation to drive away the disagreeable Bishop e5 by (5) P-f4, a move which had to be followed up with the advance of the e-Pawn who otherwise would have remained very weak, not being protected by another Pawn. The game went on as follows: (5) . . ., B-c7; (6) P-e4, B-b6+; (7) K-h1, Rf8-d8; (8) B-b1, Ra8-c8; (9) Rxd8+, Qxd8; (10) R-d1, Q-e7; (11) P-e5. This opens again the diagonal of the King's

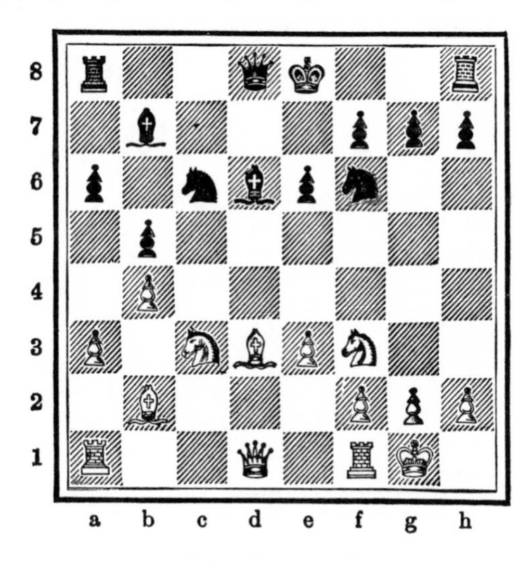

DIAGRAM 55

Bishop, but it closes that of the Queen's Bishop, and it is the advantage of the work done by his Queen's Bishop in the unobstructed diagonal which secures Black the victory. (11) . . ., Kt-d5; (12) Ktxd5, Bxd5; (13) Q-g4, Q-b7; (14) P-f5, R-c4; (15) Q-g3, R-f4 !. White cannot capture the Rook on account of Bxg2 mate. (16) P-f6, P-g6. There is now no defense against R-f2 which attacks g2 and b2 at the same time. (17) B-a2, R-f2; (18) Bxd5, Qxd5 ! and White resigns as he loses his Bishop on account of the mating threat.

It remains to examine typical middle-game maneuvers with the Queen and with the Pawns. Little is to be said about the Queen. On account of her tremendous mobility she is liable at any time to initiate a dangerous attack in conjunction with one or more of the other pieces, and most of the examples given for the typical Rook's, Bishop's and Knight's maneuvers have also shown the methods by which the co-operation with the Queen can be effected. The main field of action for the Queen is the side on which the opponent has castled. In games, in which both players have castled on the same side of the board, and which, as stated previously, constitute the vast majority of cases it is dangerous to make excursions with the Queen to distant regions away from the King, as her retreat might be cut off, making impossible an adequate defense against an attack which the opponent might be able

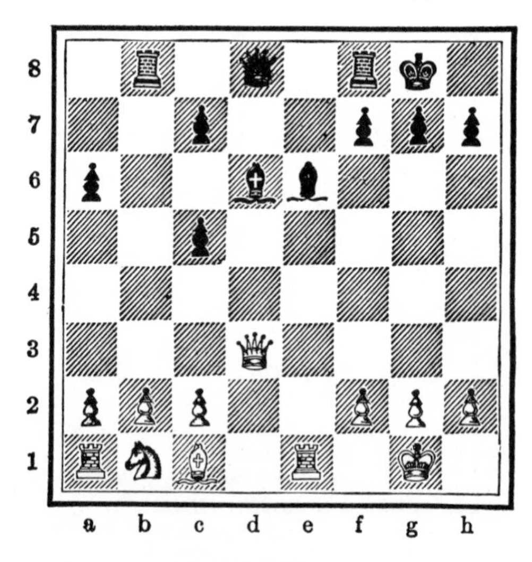

DIAGRAM 56

to initiate on the King's side with the help of his own Queen. In the position of Diagram 56 for instance, it would be very risky for White to take the Pawn a6. Black would play P-c4, cutting off the retreat of White's Queen, and then start a violent attack with his Queen in conjunction with the two Bishops. Another example is the position of Diagram 57 which occurred in a game between Capablanca and Bernstein in the San Sebastian Tournament 1911. White played (1) Kt-e2 and Black, in view of the threatening accumulation of white pieces on the King's wing, should not have risked to capture the Pawn a2, getting his Queen quite out of play. He underestimated the danger and lost the game very quickly. The attack developed as follows: (1) ..., Qxa2; (2) Kte2-g3, Qxc2. In taking the second Pawn Black loses another move. He might have tried Q-a5, threatening to exchange Queens with Q-b6. But it is doubtful whether he would have been able to save the game. White would, of course, have avoided the exchange by playing his King into the corner. (3) R-c1, Q-b2;

(4) Kt-h5; this prevents the Queen from getting back into play via f6. The threat is now R-c3, cutting Black's Queen off from g7, and then Kth5xg7 and Qxh6. Black defends himself against this threat by (4) . . ., R-h8 with the intention to answer R-c3 with K-g8; but White's position involves so many threats that Black cannot provide a

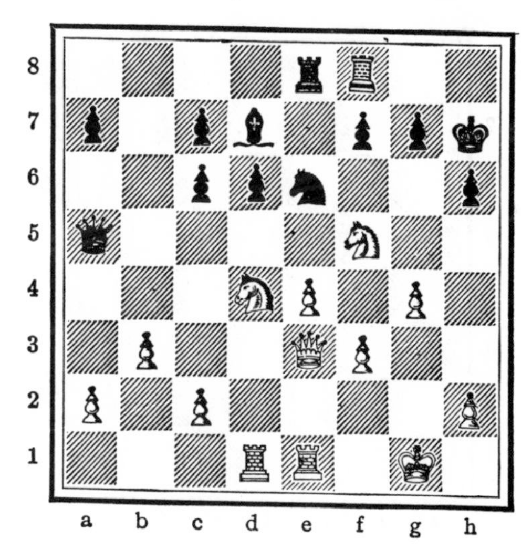

DIAGRAM 57

satisfactory protection. (5) R-e2, Q-e5; (6) P-f4, Q-b5; (7) Ktf5xg7 ! and wins, as Ktxg7 is followed by (8) Kt-f6+, (9) Ktxd7 and (10) P-f5 or P-e5 with overwhelming attack.

The most difficult problem in the conduct of the middle-game is the timely maneuvering with the Pawns. Although it is impossible to give a general rule which will apply to all cases it is a good principle to avoid Pawn moves in the middle-game just as carefully as in the opening, at least in the early stages of the middle-game. In the opening the argument against Pawn moves was the time loss connected with them from the point of view of development. In the middle-game it is mainly the weakness created by the Pawn move on the squares which were protected by the Pawn before he advanced. A square may be termed "weak" if it can be safely occupied by men which help the opponent in his attack, and this is generally possible if the square in question cannot any longer be defended by a Pawn. The great danger involved in the occupation by hostile pieces of such weak squares is evident if they are situated near the King, and examples of how the attack develops in cases of this kind have been discussed in connection with Diagram 48, 49, 50 and 52. It is less apparent why a Pawn move should create a weakness if a center-Pawn or a Pawn on the Queen's wing is concerned. In the latter case, the possibility of deriving an advantage during the

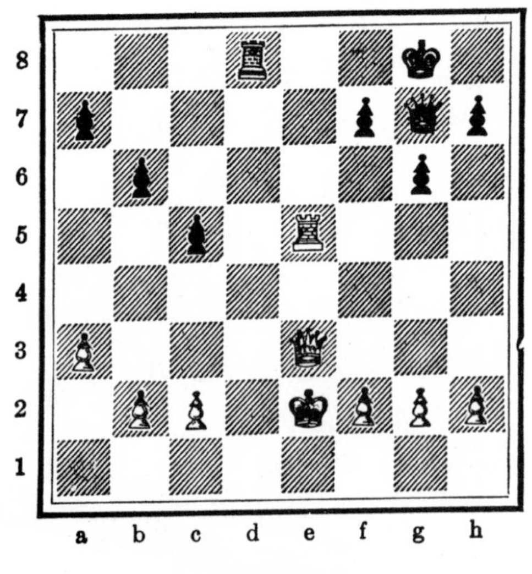

DIAGRAM 58

middle-game is rare, indeed; but the weakness produced by the Pawn moves invariably shows itself in the ending. In the position of Diagram 58 for instance, White wins on account of the weakness of the squares a6, c6, d5 and b5 from which his King can attack the Black Pawns as soon as the Queen and the Rook are exchanged. The following play may ensue: (1) R-e8+, Rxe8; (2) Qxe8+, Q-f8; (3) Qxf8+, Kxf8; (4) K-d3, K-e7; (5) K-c4, K-d7; (6) K-b5, K-c7; (7) K-a6, K-b8; (8) P-a4, K-a8; (9) P-a5, Pxa5; (10) Kxa5 and wins the c-Pawn. Or: (5) . . ., P-a6; (6) K-d5, K-d7. For the time being Black has the opposition so that White's King cannot advance any further; but White has so many more Pawn moves at his disposal than Black that the latter is soon forced to move his King allowing White to break in with his King at one or the other side. For instance: (7) P-a4, P-a5; (8) P-f4, P-f6; (9) P-g4, P-h6; (10) P-h3, P-g5; (11) P-f5; King moves, and White wins either the f-Pawn or the b-Pawn.

This example brings out another reason why it is advantageous to keep the Pawns of the wings back. In the ending positions frequently arise in which it is important to have some moves to spare in order to be able to maintain the opposition of Kings; and the player whose Pawns are farther back naturally has more spare moves.

A disadvantage which is liable to make itself felt in the middle-game as well as in Rooks' endings as a consequence of Pawn moves on the wing is the opening of an adjoining file for a hostile Rook, as illustrated by the play in the positions of Diagrams 50, 51 and 54. In the middle-game this is also true of certain Pawns, as for instance in the following position which arises after the opening moves (1) P-e4, P-e5; (2) Kt-f3, Kt-c6; (3) P-d4, Pxd4; (4) B-c4, Kt-f6; (5) o-o, B-e7. The proper

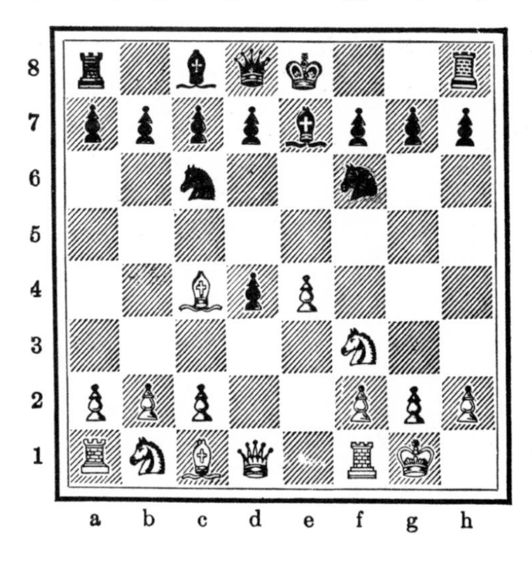

DIAGRAM 59

continuation is (6) R-e1, protecting the center-Pawn. The advance of this Pawn is entirely uncalled for. Not only does it enable Black to open the f-file for his Rook by advancing his f-Pawn, but it gives up the greatest advantage connected with the possession of a center-Pawn, that is the control of two center-squares. As long as White has his Pawn on e4, the two squares f5 and d5 are inaccessible to black pieces; as soon as the Pawn advances, however, he does not do Black any further harm, as the two squares which he controls after the advance are firmly in Black's hands on account of the two Pawns f7 and d7. A game played with this opening proceeded as follows: (6) P-e5, Kt-e4; (7) B-d5, Kt-c5;

(8) Ktxd4, Ktxd4; (9) Qxd4, 0-0; (10) Kt-c3, P-d6; (11) B-e3, P-c6; (12) B-b3, P-d5; (13) Ra1-d1, K-h8; (14) Q-f4, P-f6. This decides the middle-game in Black's favor. Not only will he have superior mobility with his Rooks, but his two Bishops are much stronger than White's two minor pieces, especially as White's Bishop is shut in. Moreover, Black has the better chances even in the ending, as he has a majority of Pawns on the Queen's wing. After all pieces have been exchanged, these Pawns would finally result in a passed Pawn, which White would have to stop with his King while Black can leisurely attack the Pawns of the King's side.

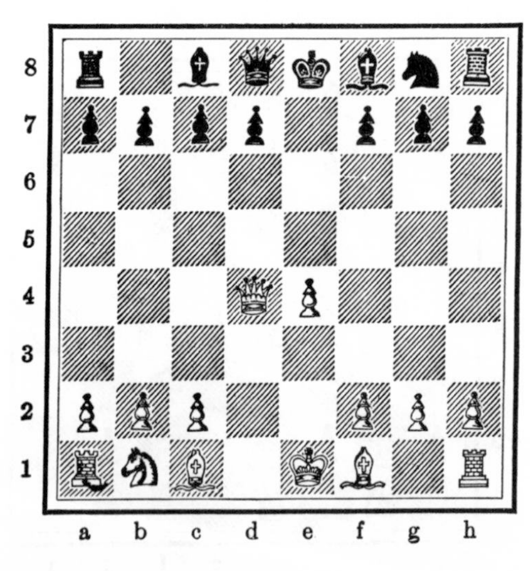

DIAGRAM 60

A disadvantage due to Pawn moves which up to now has not yet been discussed is the weakness of so-called "backward Pawns." A backward Pawn is one whose adjoining kindred Pawns have advanced while he is unable himself to advance far enough to obtain their protection from a frontal or diagonal attack. In the position of Diagram 60, for instance, Black would make his Queen's Pawn backward if he played P-c5; for if White handles the game right Black will never be able to advance the Queen's Pawn beyond d6, making him an easy mark for an attack in the d-file or in the diagonal h2-b8, and also hampering the mobility of Black's pieces in the center. The correct way for White to arrange his men would be to play P-c4 and after the development of the minor pieces to double the Rooks in the d-file. White's Queen's Bishop will be placed best on f4 from where he helps pressing on d6.

Diagram 61 shows a position which occurred in one of the match games played between Emanuel Lasker and S. Tarrasch for the World's

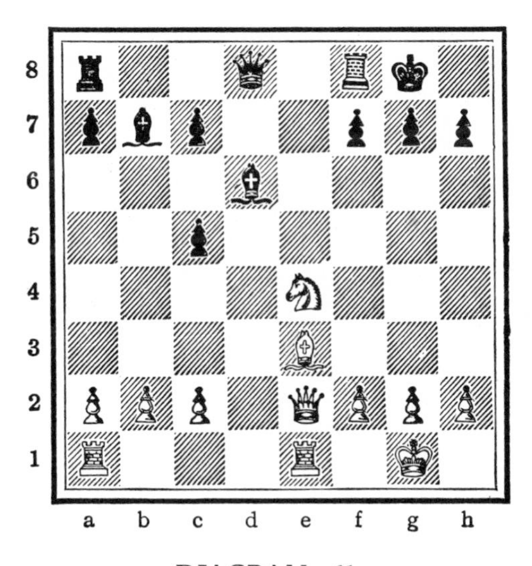

DIAGRAM 61

Championship in 1908, and which furnishes a good illustration of the difficulties arising from a backward Pawn. The game proceeded as follows: (1) Ktxd6, Pxd6; (2) Ra1-d1, Q-f6; (3) P-c4, Rf8-e8; (4) Q-g4 (threatening Q-d7) B-c6; (5) R-e2, R-e4; (6) Q-g3, Q-e6 (threatening R-g4); (7) P-h3, R-d8. Black cannot protect the Pawn d6 as many times as White can attack him. It looks as if he could have taken the Pawn c4 with his Queen, but he was probably afraid of the weakness White would have provoked with B-h6, (8) Re2-d2, Re4-e5; (9) B-h6 ! Black cannot take the Bishop on account of Qxe5. (9) . . ., Q-g6; (10) B-f4 and wins, as the Pawn d6 as well as the Pawn c5 are doomed.

In a position like that of Diagram 45 on page 76 White could play P-f4 without making his King's Pawn backward, as neither a frontal nor a diagonal attack on e3 is possible. Of course, he would have to see that the possibility of such an attack does not arise later on. For instance, he would not be in a position to take the Pawn c5 with the

Pawn d4, as this would enable Black to use the diagonal a7-g1 for operations against e3.

The player who endeavors to adhere in all positions to the principles of Chess Strategy outlined in this chapter will rapidly improve his strength and acquire within a short time a much more intimate grasp of the game than others who have had years of practice without making clear to themselves the general laws which govern the outcome of every combination on the Chessboard.

The illustrative games analyzed in the following chapter do not reach anything new. They are merely examples of the application of the general principles to the continuous series of combinations which constitute a game of Chess. The author has chosen games from his own tournament practice as this naturally enabled a more thorough annotation than would have been possible to offer for games of other players.

IV

ILLUSTRATIVE GAMES

GAME No. 1

Played in the Championship Tournament of the Western States, 1917, at Lexington, Ky.

	White	Black
	Jackson Showalter	*Edward Lasker*
(1)	P-e4	P-e5
(2)	Kt-f3	Kt-c6
(3)	B-b5	P-a6

As explained previously this move cannot be regarded as loss of time as White has to either retreat with the Bishop, adding nothing to his development, or exchange on c6, helping Black's development by opening a line for the Bishop c8.

(4) B-a4 Kt-f6

The move B-c5 which Black might consider instead of Kt-f6 is not to be recommended as White would reply P-c3 and then force the exchange of Black's center-Pawn by P-d4. The complete control of the center which White would gain in the further course of the game would soon give him an overwhelming attack. For instance: (4) . . ., B-c5; (5) P-c3, Kt-f6; (6) o-o, o-o; (7) P-d4, Pxd4; (8) Pxd4, B-b6; (9) P-e5, Kt-e8; (10) P-d5, Kt-e7; (11) P-d6, Pxd6; (12) Pxd6, Kt-g6; (13) B-g5, etc.

(5) P-d3

It is customary for White to castle at this point. P-d3 is certainly a good move as it enables the development of the Queen's Bishop, but o-o is very likely better as it reserves the option of advancing the Queen's Pawn either one or two squares. When advancing the Pawn two squares White has to avoid the following trap: (5) o-o, B-e7; (6) P-d4, P-b5; (7) B-b3, Pxd4 (not Ktxd4 on account of (8) Bxf7+ and (9) Ktxe5+); (8) Ktxd4 ??, Ktxd4; (9) Qxd4, P-c5 followed by P-c4 winning the Bishop. What White can try in this variation is the Pawn sacrifice (8) P-c3, Pxc3, through which he obtains a considerable advantage in the development of the pieces.

After (5) o-o White threatens to win the Pawn e5 by (6) Bxc6 and (7) Ktxe5, as now Q-d4; (8) Kt-f3, Qxe4 is not possible on account of (9) R-e1. Black has various ways to counter this threat. He can

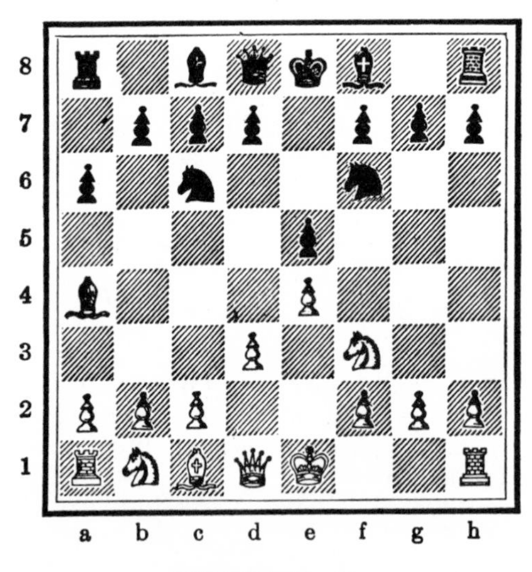

DIAGRAM 62

either defend the Pawn by P-d6 or play B-e7 with the view to capture the Pawn e4 in case White should take the Pawn e5, or, finally, he can capture the Pawn e4 at once.

All of these three variations are playable for Black although it appears that White obtains a slight advantage however Black continues. This opening is consequently a great favorite in modern Tournament play.[1]

(5) . . . P-b5

[1] Following are the two main variations which have been adopted in the practice of the Masters:

A. (5) o-o, B-e7; (6) R-e1 (protecting the Pawn e4 so that Black has to defend himself against Bxc6 and Ktxe5), P-b5; (7) B-b3, P-d6; (8) P-c3 (preserving the Bishop against the exchange threatened with Kt-a5), Kt-a5; (9) B-c2, P-c5; (10) P-d4, Q-c7. Now the Pawn e5 is sufficiently protected and Black threatens to exert pressure on d4 by playing B-g4 and Kt-c6. It might seem that White can ignore this threat and as soon as d4 attacked either exchange the Pawn on e5 or advance him to d5. However, the former maneuver would open the d-file for Black's Rooks and the latter would not be very good either before Black has castled; for the advance of the d-pawn closes the

The simplest and probably best way to defend the Pawn e5 against the threat Bxc6 and Ktxe5 is P-d6 without P-b5.

(6) B-b3 P-d6

The alternative was B-c5. White could then not have captured the

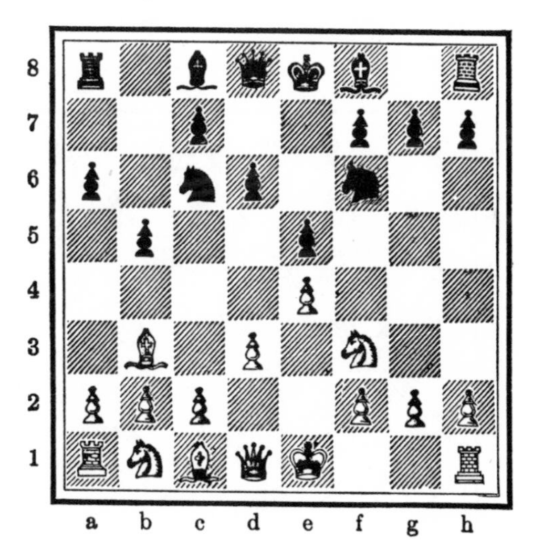

DIAGRAM 63

Pawn e5 by (7) B-d5, o-o; (8) Bxc6, Pxc6; (9) Ktxe5 on account of Q-d4, threatening mate on f2 and attacking the Knight.

(7) Kt-g5

center-files permanently for the Rooks so that Black's King is safe in the center while White may have to face an attack on the King's wing which Black might initiate by storming with the h and g Pawns.

For all these reasons White is justified in making the waiting move (11) P-h3, which safeguards the square d4 against the indirect attack B-g4 and at the same time prepares an attack along the lines of the one discussed in connection with Diagram 52. After (11) . . ., Kt-c6; (12) B-e3, o-o; White can safely advance the Queen's Pawn and then launch the attack referred to above.

B. The second variation arising from the position of Diagram 62 is (5) o-o, Ktxe4. It seems rather dangerous for Black to take the Pawn as long as his King is in the e-file which White can occupy with his Rook; but after (6) R-e1, Kt-c5; (7) Ktxe5, Ktxe5; (8) Rxe5+, Kt-e6, White has not much attack and for this reason the opening is generally treated in a different way. As the strongest move is considered (6) P-d4. Black can hardly take this Pawn as R-e1 and Ktxd4 would follow threatening to win a piece; but he may try to maintain his Knight on the dominating square e4 by (6)

This attack with two pieces in the early stage of the opening is contrary to the general principles of strategy. White wins a Pawn but this cannot be considered an adequate equivalent for the time he loses in doing so. He neglects his development and he is bound to suffer for that sooner than he can make the weight of his extra-Pawn felt.

(7) . . . P-d5
(8) Pxd5

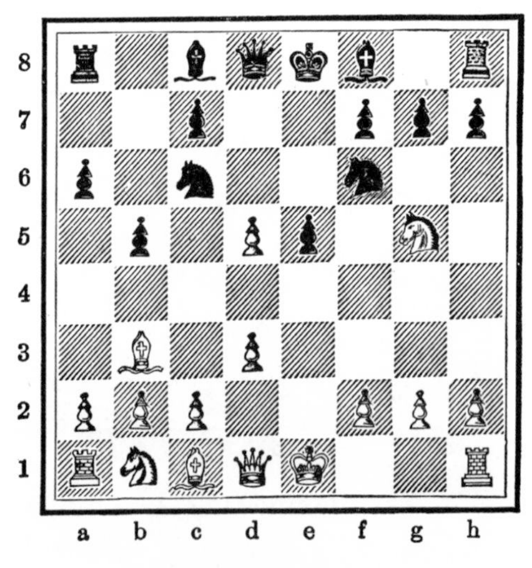

DIAGRAM 64

Black cannot recapture the Pawn as this would give White an occasion to initiate a violent attack starting with the sacrifice of the Knight on f7, thus: (8) . . ., Ktxd5; (9) Ktxf7, Kxf7; (10) Q-f3+, K-e6 (the Knight d5 has to be protected); (11) Kt-c3, Ktc6-e7; (12) o-o, followed

. . ., P-b5; (7) B-b3, P-d5. After (8) Pxe5, B-e6; (9) P-c3 (again providing a retreat for the Bishop), B-e7; (10) Ktb1-d2, Black's best continuation is probably Ktxd2; (11) Qxd2 (not Bxd2 on account of B-g4); Kt-a5 or o-o. The maneuver (10) . . ., Kt-c5; (11) B-c2, P-d4, which was tried in several recent tournaments, is of doubtful value as Black loses control of the important center-square e4. White can use this square for an attack on the weak point c6 as follows: (12) Kt-e4, Pxc3; (13) Ktxc5, Bxc5; (14) B-e4, Q-d7; (15) Q-c2, B-d5 (in order to answer R-d1 with Bxe4); (16) B-g5, and Black does not seem to have a satisfactory defense. For instance (16) . . ., B-b6; (17) Ra1-d1, Bxe4; (18) Qxe4, Q-e6; (19) R-d6 or (16) . . ., Bxe4; (17) Qxe4, Pxb2; (18) Ra1-d1, P-b1 (Q); (19) Rxb1 followed by R-c1.

by R-e1, P-d4, etc. The exposed position of Black's King is well worth the piece which White has sacrificed.

(8) . . . Kt-d4

With this move Black crosses White's plans by exchanging the Bishop who was to play the main part in the attack, and, as a consequence, the Knight g5 does not have a chance to do any useful work either.

(9) P-d6

Opening again the diagonal of the Bishop and getting rid of the advanced Pawn by exchange before Black has an occasion to capture him.

(9) . . . Ktxb3
(10) Pxc7 Qxc7

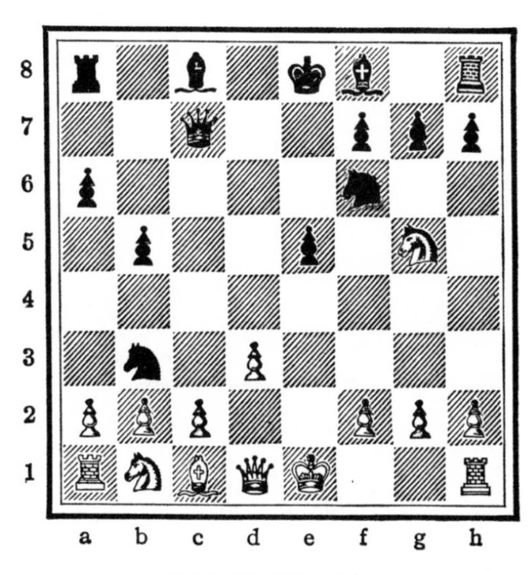

DIAGRAM 65

Black could regain his Pawn by Q-d5; (11) Pa2xb3, Qxg2; (12) Q-f3, Qxf3; (13) Ktxf3, B-b7; (14) K-e2, B-d6 and Bxc7; but in doing so he would give up his advantage in development, which, as the further course of the game proves, is much more valuable.

(11) Pa2xb3 B-b7
(12) 0-0 P-h6!

If Black proceeded to develop his pieces indiscriminately, his advantage would soon vanish. White needs only two moves—R-e1 and Kt-e4—to paralyze the effect of Black's powerful Queen's Bishop and to regain control of the center where at present Black has the upper hand on account of his center-Pawn.

(13)	Kt-f3	B-d6
(14)	R-e1	0-0
(15)	Ktb1-d2	Ra8-d8
(16)	P-c3	

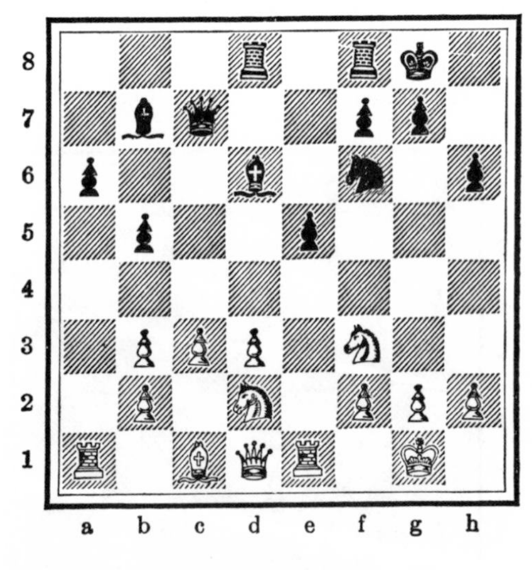

DIAGRAM 66

White does not risk Kt-e4 as Black, after Ktxe4; (17) Pxe4, can uncover the Rook by B-b4 attacking White's Queen and Rook at the same time. White's only defense would be (18) B-d2 or Kt-d2, but he would pin himself badly in either case and Black would obtain an overwhelming attack by P-f5, which enables his King's Rook to join the fray.

With P-c3 White protects himself against B-b4 and now actually threatens to interrupt the diagonal of Black's Queen's Bishop. Black will naturally try to prevent this and the first move which presents itself for the purpose is P-e4, opening a line for the Bishop d6 and the Queen at the same time. At first sight the move does not seem playable as on e4 the Pawn is three times attacked and only twice defended; but

White cannot withdraw both the Knight d2 and the Pawn d3 from the Queen's file on account of the threat Bxh2+ winning the Queen for Rook and Bishop. Black can, therefore, safely advance the Pawn.

(16) . . .	P-e4
(17) Pxe4	Ktxe4
(18) Q-c2	

Now that the Queen has left the d-file, unpinning the Knight, something must be done for the Knight e4 who is thrice attacked and only once protected. Two moves come into consideration. One is P-f5 which maintains the Knight in the dominating center-position, as White cannot take him without opening the f-file for Black's Rook and losing the Pawn h2 who needs the protection of the Knight f3. The other is Ktxd2, winning the Pawn h2 right away no matter whether White retakes with the Bishop or with the Knight. Which of the two moves is the better is difficult to say and is more or less a matter of temperament. A player who prefers a slow and sure advance will choose P-f5. A player who likes a faster pace will start the hand-to-hand fight without delay by Ktxd2. It is the latter move on which Black decides.

(18) . . .	Ktxd2

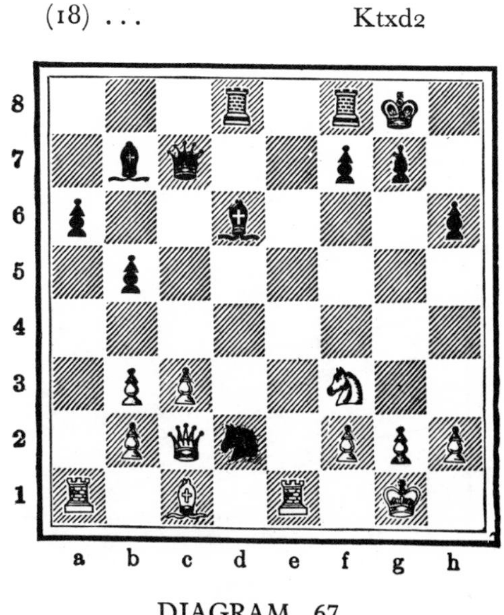

DIAGRAM 67

White now faces the dilemma whether to recapture with the Bishop or with the Knight. If he takes with the Bishop Black exchanges on f3, breaking up White's chain of Pawns, and he regains his Pawn by Bxh2. If he takes with the Knight, Black also wins the Pawn h2, but the other Pawns in front of the King remain intact. The drawback to the latter continuation is, however, that White's development is delayed for another two moves, as the Queen's Bishop is shut in. For this reason White decides on Bxd2, probably also hoping that he will be compensated for the broken Pawn position by an attack in the g- or h-file which Black's maneuver opens.

(19) Bxd2 Bxf3

The fact that Black has to exchange his well placed Queen's Bishop in order to win the Pawn h2 was very likely another reason which induced White to retake with the Bishop.

(20) Pxf3 Bxh2+
(21) K-g2

A general survey of the position shows clearly that Black has the advantage. His Rook d8 is ready to take part in the battle while White has to make several preparatory moves with his Rooks before he can make

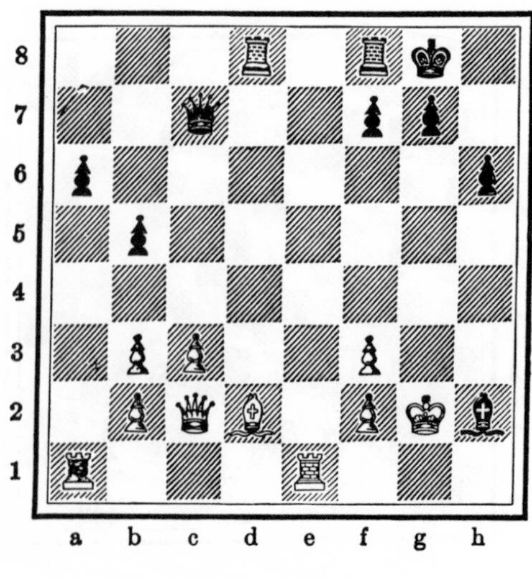

DIAGRAM 68

use of them on the King's wing, the only part of the board where they have a chance to be effective. In the e-line which White's Rook controls at present, there is no tangible object for an attack.

Moreover, White's King is rather exposed while Black's King is safely entrenched behind his Pawns.

A good continuation for Black, which presents itself at first thought, is R-d6, enabling the doubling of the Rooks in the d-line or the participation of the Rook d6 in a fight on the King's wing.

(21) ...	R-d6
(22) R-e4	

White cannot take the Bishop h2 as Rxd2+ would win the Queen. (22) P-f4 would not be good either as Black would reply Q-d7, threatening Rxd2 as well as Q-g4+; Kxh2, R-g6 and mate in two moves.

With R-e4 White attempts to protect his King by R-g4 against attacks in the g-file, and Black naturally tries to foil this attempt.

(22) ...	P-f5
(23) R-h4	

Black has now to decide whether he should withdraw his Bishop to e5 or counterattack White's Bishop by Q-d7 or Q-d8 or Rf8-d8. The counterattack looks better as it threatens to force an entrance for the Rooks in the second rank, displacing White's Queen and attacking the King from the flank. The withdrawal of the Bishop would give White time to play his Queen's Rook over to the King's wing.

The most forcible of the three moves available for the counterattack is Q-d8, which attacks the Rook h4 too, thereby depriving White of the possibility to save his Bishop by flight.

(23) ...	Q-d8
(24) Rxh2	Rxd2
(25) Q-c1	

White's Queen has now hardly any mobility and in addition she shuts off the Queen's Rook from the King's wing. Black, on the other hand, can easily get his Rooks to coöperate by doubling them either in the d-file or in the second rank. He decides on the former alternative because the control of the Queen's file keeps White's troops separated in two parts which have little or no communication with each other, while Black's pieces are ready for concentration on the King's wing at any moment.

(25)	...	Q-g5+
(26)	K-h1	Rf8-d8
(27)	Q-e1	

With the intention to play Q-e6+, thereby gaining time to swing over the Queen's Rook to the King's wing.

(27)	...	K-h7
(28)	Q-c1	

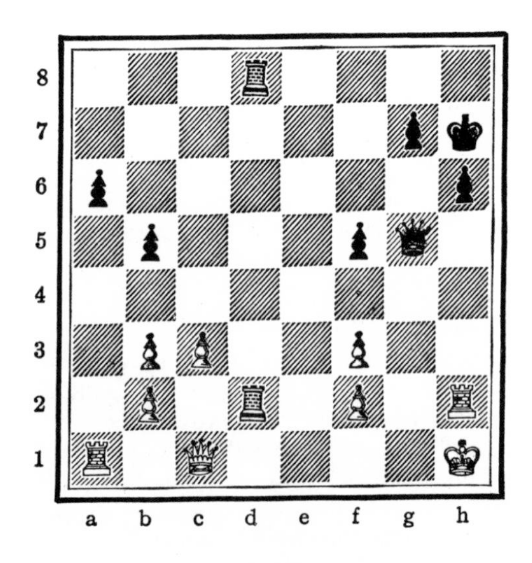

DIAGRAM 69

The Queen cannot leave the first rank on account of the threat R-d1+. It lies near for Black to try to force her out by attacking the square d1 once more with the Queen, thereby threatening to win the Queen for a Rook by the check on d1. He can accomplish this by playing the Queen into the d-file behind the Rooks.

(28)	...	Rd8-d6
(29)	P-c4	

(29) Q-g1 would have offered a little longer resistance, though Qxg1 + followed by Rxb2 would have led to a hopeless ending with two Pawns down. The reply (29) . . . , Q-d8, however, would have left White with a faint drawing chance: (30) R-g2, R-d1 ?; (31) Rxg7 +,

K-h8; (32) R-g8 + !, etc. By moving his Bishop's Pawn White saves his Queen but exposes his King to an immediately fatal assault.

(29) . . . Q-d8
(30) Q-c3

Black now enforces a mate in ten moves: R-d1 +; (31) Rxd1, Rxd1 +; (32) K-g2, Q-g5+; (33) K-h3, R-g1; (34) Q-d4, Q-h5+; (35) Q-h4, Qxf3+; (36) Q-g3, Rxg3+; (37) Pxg3, P-f4; (38) K-h4, Qxg3+; (39) K-h5, Q-g5 mate. This instructive game was not lost through a faulty combination but on account of loss of time in the opening which could not be regained.

GAME No. 2

Played in the New York Masters' Tournament, 1915

White	*Black*
Edward Lasker	*Jose Raoul Capablanca*
(1) P-d4	P-d5
(2) Kt-f3	Kt-f6
(3) P-c4	P-e6
(4) Kt-c3	Ktb8-d7
(5) B-g5	B-b4

Ordinarily the Bishop is developed to e7 as on b4 he is out of place as soon as White has castled.

(6) P-e3 P-c5

With this move Black threatens Q-a5, attacking the Knight c3 for the second time and unpinning the Knight f6 who is then free to coöperate with the Bishop b4 and the Queen by advancing to e4. In trying to counter Black's threat White will seek to do as much as he can for the development of his pieces so as to combine the attack with defense. The King's Bishop is not yet developed, and his most natural developing move happens to cover the square at which Black is aiming with his Knight.

(7) B-d3 Q-a5
(8) Q-b3

White has to be very careful on account of the various exchanges possible in the center. Black threatens for instance to exchange first on d4 and then to play Kt-e4 so that the Bishop g5 is attacked by the Queen in case White takes the Knight with his Bishop, allowing the Pawn d5 to clear the fifth rank. Or he might play Kt-e4 first and then exchange on d4. Considering that all these threats are based on the fact that the Knight c3 is pinned as long as White has not yet castled it lies near for White to try (8) o-o. It is true that Black can then win a Pawn by taking twice on c3; however, in doing so he would retard his

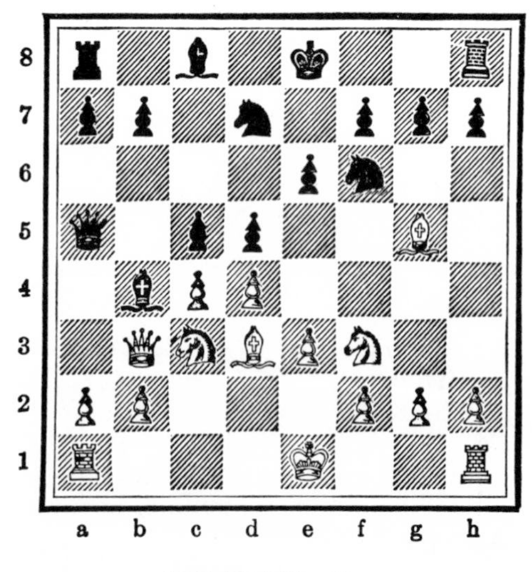

DIAGRAM 70

development and White is bound to obtain a strong attack by getting all of his pieces quickly into action, while Black's Queen is separated from the rest of her troops.

White's eighth move, Q-b3, has several drawbacks. First of all Black could play P-b5! winning a piece for three Pawns as White cannot do better than play (9) Pxb5 or Pxd5 allowing P-c4. Secondly, Black can make the combination indicated above which tends to open the fifth rank so that the Queen attacks g5. The same combination would be possible if White played (8) Q-c2.

(8) . . .	Kt-e4
(9) o-o	

Offering the Pawn sacrifice Ktxc3; (10) Pxc3, Bxc3 with the view to attacking by (11) R-c1, etc., as previously indicated. Black prefers to direct his attack against g5.

(9)	...	Ktxg5
(10)	Ktxg5	Pxd4
(11)	Kt-b5	

(11) Pxd4 would lose a piece on account of Pxc4, attacking the Bishop on d3 and the Knight on g5. Black could now win a Pawn by taking on e3, but this would be very dangerous as it would open the f-file for White's Rook.

(11)	...	Kt-c5

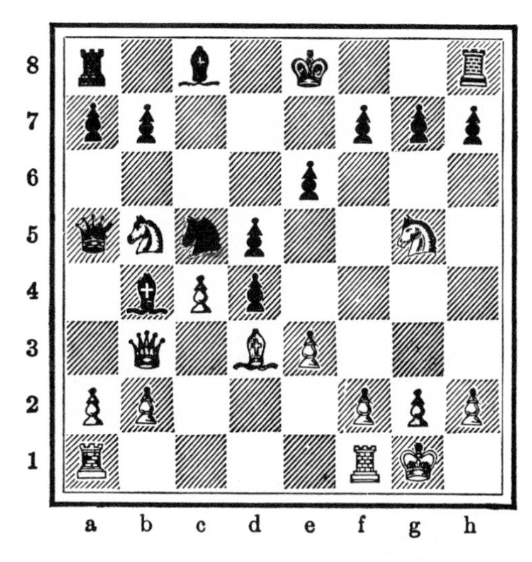

DIAGRAM 71

The position is getting very complicated indeed. The first possibility which White will consider is (12) Kt-d6+; but after K-e7 there seems to be no satisfactory continuation. For instance: (13) Q-c2, Ktxd3; (14) Ktd6xf7, R-f8 winning two Knights for the Rook. Or: (14) Ktxc8+ ?, Ra8xc8; (15) Qxd3, Pxc4 winning a piece. Therefore, White has no alternative but to retire the Queen.

(12)	Q-c2	Ktxd3
(13)	Qxd3	P-a6

It is not easy for Black to retain the Pawn which he has won. If he plays (13) . . ., B-e7; (14) Kt-f3, Pxe3; White can continue (15) Pxd5 with good attacking chances on account of the open files in the center of the board, of which Black cannot yet make any use as he has not yet castled.

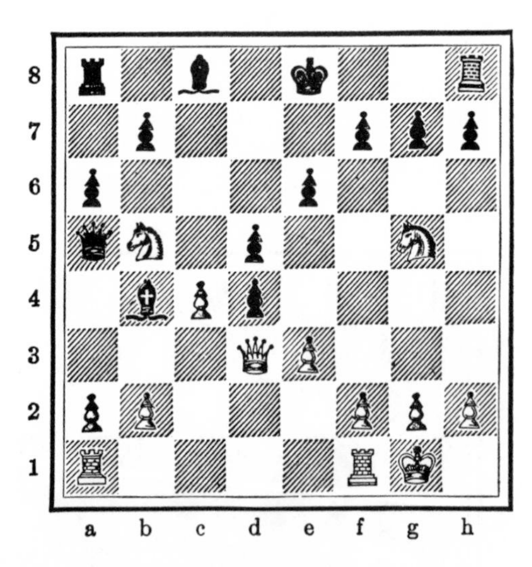

DIAGRAM 72

By P-a6 Black opens again the fifth rank in order to operate against the Knight g5.

(14)	Ktxd4	Pxc4
(15)	Qxc4	B-d7
(16)	Kt-b3	

A very bad move, as it violates the general principles of strategy. In withdrawing the Knight from the dominating center square White decreases his mobility instead of increasing it. The logical continuation would have been Rf1-d1 or Ra1-c1, developing one of the Rooks.

(16)	. . .	Qxg5
(17)	Qxb4	B-c6

Black would not have been able to occupy this favorable square with his Bishop, had not White withdrawn his Knight from d4.

(18)	P-e4	P-a5

This forces the Queen out of the diagonal a3-f8 as the Pawn e4 has to be kept protected.

(19) Q-d2 Qxd2

Black demonstrates in a very simple manner that the exchange of

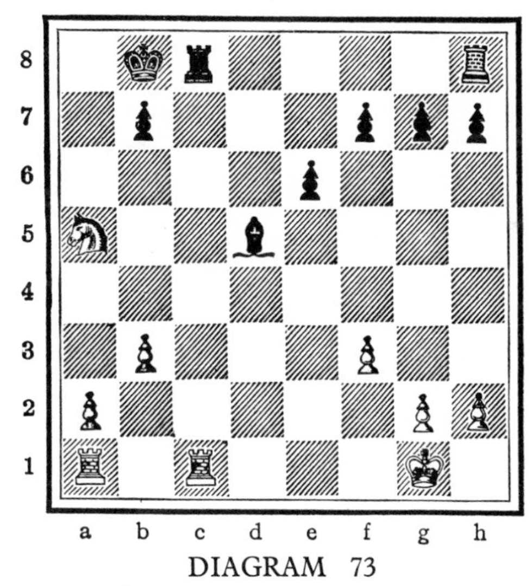

DIAGRAM 73
Position after White's 25th move.

Queens is disadvantageous for White, a fact that White should have foreseen as the unprotected Knight on d2 enables Black to gain control of the d-file by castling on the Queen's side.

(20) Ktxd2 0-0-0
(21) Kt-c4

White cannot play R-d1 on account of R-d4, threatening Rh8-d8.

(21) . . . Bxe4
(22) Rf1-c1

This merely drives the Black King to a safe place. Ktxa5 was indicated. R-d2 could then have been answered by (23) R-c1+ and (24) R-c4.

(22) . . . K-b8
(23) P-f3

Again a move which helps the opponent as it drives the Bishop where he wants to go.

(23)	...	B-d5
(24)	Ktxa5	R-c8
(25)	P-b3	

This situation furnishes an instructive example of the importance of the rules governing Pawn formations as previously discussed. By attacking the Knight with the King, Black can force the exchange of the Bishop for the Knight on c4. This leaves White with a Pawn on c4 who is weak on account of his advanced position. Black can attack him with the King and White's King is consequently compelled to stay on the Queen's wing guarding the Pawn, while Black is at leisure to secure a passed Pawn on the King's wing. These maneuvers are, of course, possible only with the Rooks off the board. That is why Black tries to force their exchange and why White should endeavor to prevent it.

(25)	...	Rxc1+
(26)	Rxc1	R-c8
(27)	Rxc8+	

In view of the hopeless Pawn ending it would have been best to give up a Pawn by (27) R-d1, P-b6; (28) Kt-c4, Bxc4; (29) Pxc4, Rxc4; (30) R-d2 in order to keep a Rook on the board, thus obtaining a drawing chance.

(27)	...	Kxc8
(28)	K-f2	K-c7
(29)	K-e3	K-b6
(30)	Kt-c4+	Bxc4
(31)	Pxc4	K-c5
(32)	K-d3	P-e5

Black's strategy in this ending is clearly indicated. He will play P-f5 and advance the e-Pawn as soon as White plays K-c3. Instead of the latter move White could play P-a3 which would also keep Black's King from b4; but he would soon run out of spare moves with his Pawns necessitating a King's move. For instance, (32) P-a3, P-f5; (33) P-g4, P-g6; (34) P-h3, P-h6; (35) P-h4, P-h5; (36) P-g5, P-b6 !; (37) K-c3, P-e4; (38) P-f4, P-e3; (39) K-d3, P-e2; (40) Kxe2, Kxc4; (41) K-e3, P-b5. Black needs now only six moves to queen the Pawn b5 while White in the meantime cannot do more than capture the g- and h-Pawns, and Black's Queen can naturally stop the White passed Pawns without difficulty.

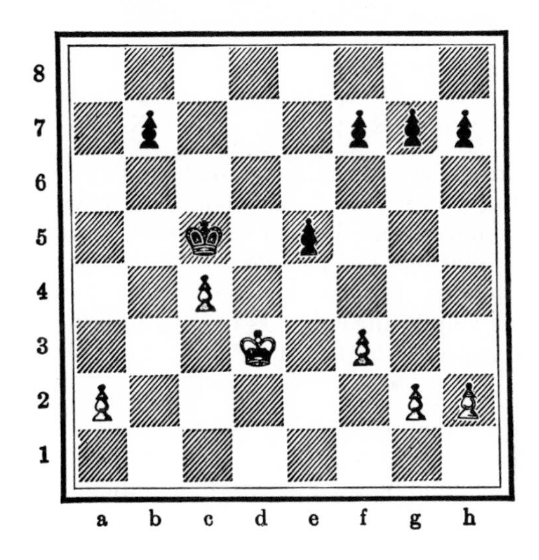

DIAGRAM 74

Position after the 32nd move.

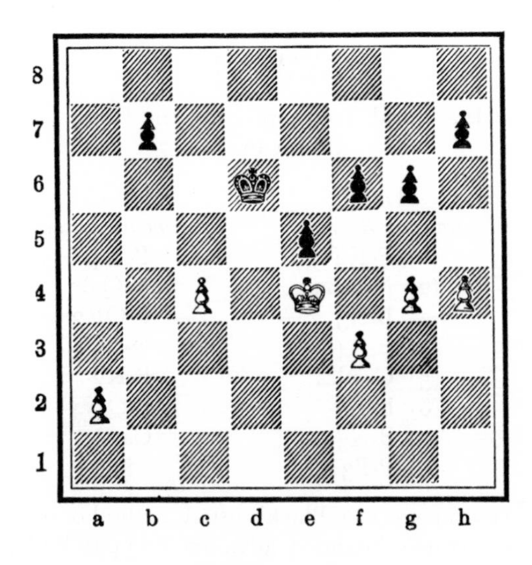

DIAGRAM 75

Position after the 35th move.

The game proceeded as follows:

(33)	P-g4	P-f6
(34)	P-h4	P-g6
(35)	K-e4	K-d6

Black could just as well have captured the Pawn c4 and permitted (36) P-g5, Pxg5; (37) Pxg5. He would then have had a Queen in another eight moves while White could not get farther with his Pawn than to g7, so that Black easily wins.

To march against the Pawn b7 instead of the Pawns on the King's side would not help White either, as he does not get back to the King's wing in time to protect his f- and g-Pawns.

(36)	P-f4	Pxf4
(37)	Kxf4	K-c5
(38)	P-h5	Kxc4
(39)	K-e4	P-b5
(40)	P-a3	K-c5
(41)	Resigns.	

GAME No. 3

Played in the Inaugural Tournament of the Chess Club Capablanca at Havana, 1947

	White	*Black*
	Rosendo Romero	*Edward Lasker*
(1)	P-K4	P-K4
(2)	N-KB3	N-QB3
(3)	B-N5	P-QR3
(4)	B-R4	N-B3
(5)	Castles	B-K2
(6)	R-K1	P-QN4
(7)	B-N3	Castles
(8)	P-B3	

As explained on page 100, Black's usual method of holding his Pawn center against White's intended advance P-Q4 is P-Q3, in order to continue with B-KN5 if White does not play P-KR3 first.

In a famous game against Capablanca, played in 1918, the then U.S. champion Frank Marshall introduced an astonishing innovation at this point. He sacrificed a Pawn with (8) . . ., P-Q4 !; (9) PxP, NxP; (10) NxP, NxN; (11) RxN, N-B3, in the hope of working up a lethal attack before White could develop his Queen's wing. Capablanca weathered

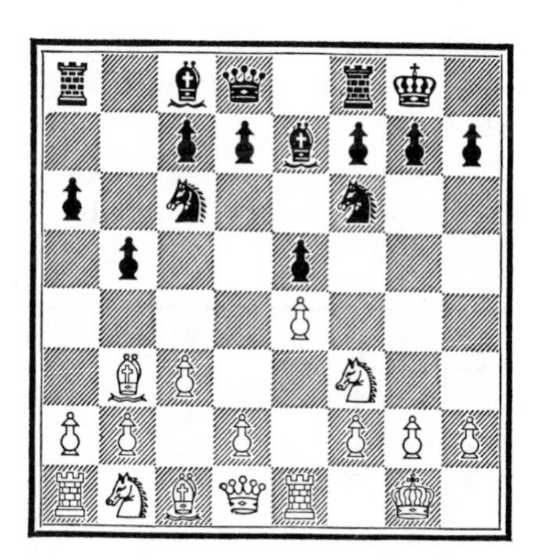

DIAGRAM 76

the storm, however, and Marshall later thought that (11) . . ., P-QB3 was Black's best continuation. He also tried the move chosen by the author in the present game, but with best play White can obtain a clear advantage.

(8)	P-Q4
(9) PxP	P-K5?

The refutation of this second Pawn sacrifice, suggested by the necessity of completing development, is (10) PxN, PxN; (11) P-Q4 ! when neither PxP; (12) Q-B3 nor other moves give Black attacking chances which compensate him for the Pawn.

The continuation adopted by Romero also poses difficult problems, but Black retains some pull.

(10) N-N5	N-K4
(11) NxKP	N-Q6
(12) NxNch	BxN

(13) R-K3 NxB?

With two Pawns down, Black should avoid exchanges. With B-B4!; (14) Q-B1, P-QB4! (and (15) PxP e.p., Q-Q3) he could have kept White bottled up.

(14) QxN B-N4

P-QB4 still would have been very strong, with the continuation (15) PxP e.p., B-N4; (16) R-K1, B-B4; (17) B-B2, B-Q6; (18) BxB, QxB; (19) N-R3, KR-Q1 !

(15) R-K1 B-N2
(16) Q-Q1 Q-B3
(17) P-Q4 Q-R3

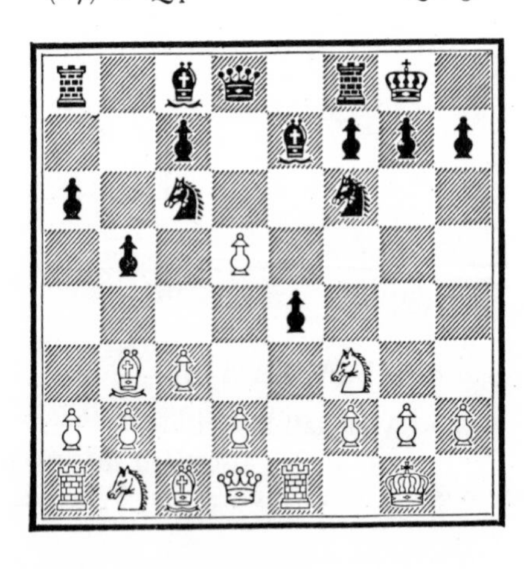

DIAGRAM 77

Position after the 9th move.

Preventing the Knight from reaching the ideal spot KB3. However, the square K3 also proves to be quite effective for the Knight.

(18) N-R3 QR-Q1
(19) N-B2 R-Q3 !

Avoiding the exchange of Bishops is much more promising than regaining one Pawn with BxP.

(20)	N-K3	P-KB4
(21)	Q-B3	B-B1
(22)	R-K2	Q-N3

In order to play P-KR4, so that the Knight cannot go to N4 when driven by P-B5.

(23)	QR-K1	P-KR4
(24)	B-B2	Q-B2
(25)	P-KR3	B-Q1

Intending P-N4. But White demonstrates clearly that the advanced Pawns are weak. P-N3, followed by B-N2, was probably the best plan.

(26)	N-B1	P-N4

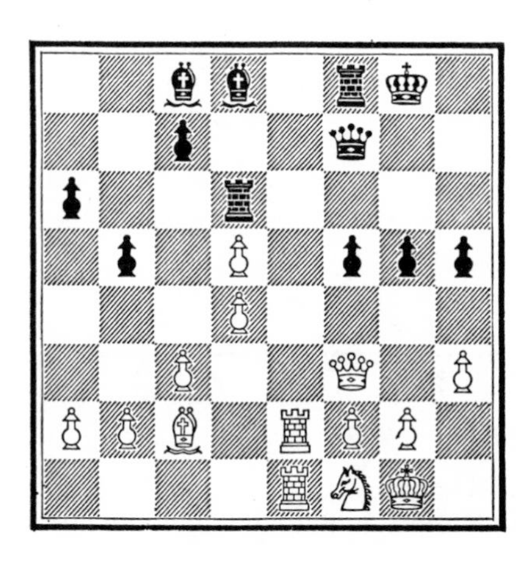

DIAGRAM 78

(27) R-K6 !

Black cannot capture twice on K3, for after BxR; (28) PxB, RxP?, White would win a piece with (29) RxR as QxR is not possible because of B-N3.

(27)	. . .	P-KN5
(28)	PxP	RPxP
(29)	Q-B4	BxR
(30)	PxB	Q-N2

The Pawn cannot be held. Q-R2 would have been answered by N-K3, threatening NxBP and also NxNP.

(31)	BxP	B-R5

Both players were pressed for time. This explains a certain aimlessness of their moves up to the fortieth turn. Black's last move invites White into a trap: (32) QxP?, BxPch!, and White cannot take the Bishop because of QxQ.

(32)	R-K5	P-N5
(33)	P-KN3	B-B3
(34)	R-K4	PxP
(35)	PxP	B-K2
(36)	P-QB4?	

The push of the center-Pawns which White undertakes is ineffective because they are forced into a white phalanx, and the black Bishop stops them from advancing further. Very likely White could have decided the game quickly by bringing the Knight into the fray via R2 and N4.

(36)	....	B-B3
(37)	P-Q5	R-QN3
(38)	QxP?	

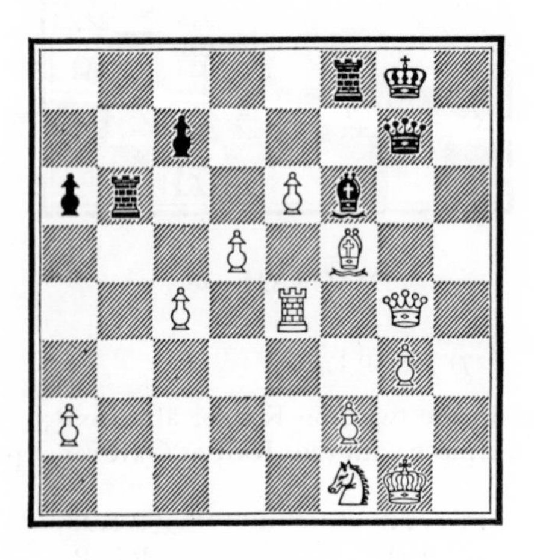

DIAGRAM 79

This removes the threat of a mating attack, and Black obtains a counter-chance on the other wing.

(38)	....	QxQ
(39)	RxQch	K-R1
(40)	R-K4	B-K2
(41)	P-N4	R-N7

Now the Rook's Pawn falls, and Black's passed Pawn is apt to become a real menace unless White can storm Black's defenses on the King's wing. This White now attempts with a sacrifice which permits his Knight quickly to get into action.

(42)	N-K3	RxRP
(43)	P-Q6 !	BxP
(44)	N-Q5	P-B3 !

The only move to stave off immediate defeat.

(45)	N-B4	BxN
(46)	P-K7	B-Q3 !

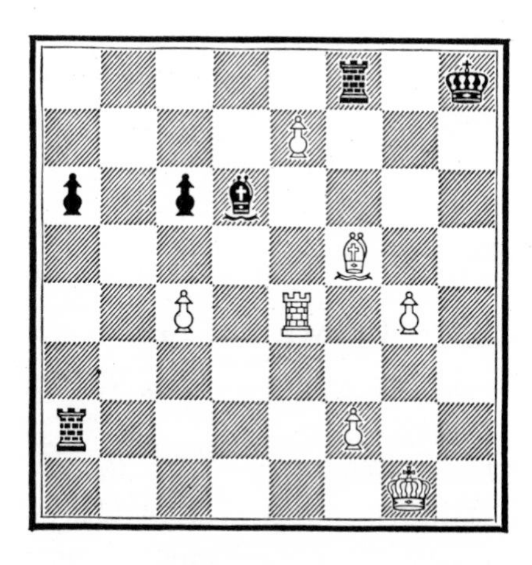

DIAGRAM 80

The ensuing end-game with Bishops of different colors offers Black a good drawing chance. White's connected passed Pawns are very dangerous, but his Rook and Bishop will be kept busy by Black's Pawn, because the latter is not blocked by White's King.

(47)	PxR(Q)ch	BxQ
(48)	B-Q7?	

This is not sufficiently aggressive. The best plan was to run with the Pawns: P-B4, P-N5, R-K8, B-K6, P-B5, etc., with good winning prospects.

(48)	. . .	P-B4
(49)	R-K6	R-Q7 !
(50)	B-B8	P-R4
(51)	R-QR6	B-N2 !

Now White cannot hold his King's Bishop's Pawn, and since his connected passed Pawns constituted his only winning chance, the game is now certain to end in a draw.

(52)	RxP	B-Q5
(53)	K-N2	RxPch
(54)	K-N3	K-N2
(55)	B-B5	R-K7
(56)	R-R6	R-K8

and White cannot force his Pawn across the black square KN7 which is doubly guarded by Black. An exciting game throughout.

GAME No. 4

Played at the Marshall Chess Club, New York, in 1947

White	Black
Edward Lasker	*J. Ayalla*
(1) P-Q4	P-Q4

In modern tournament Chess, Black rarely advances a center-Pawn to the fourth rank on the first move, but tries to hold open as long as possible the option of playing either P-K4 or P-Q4.

The reply to (1) P-Q4 is almost invariably N-KB3, and the reply to (1) P-K4 either N-KB3 or P-QB4 or P-K3.

(2)	P-K3	P-K3
(3)	QN-Q2	

This move, too, is motivated by the desire to maintain a choice among several openings. White may lead either into a Queen's Gambit with P-QB4, or he may adopt the "Colle system" or related lines, in which the Queen's Bishop's Pawn is kept on the third rank and all pieces are played over to the King's wing, as in the present game.

(3) ...	N-KB3
(4) B-Q3	P-B4
(5) P-QB3	QN-Q2
(6) P-KB4	

White now controls his own as well as Black's square K5. As a consequence, Black will not be able to advance his King's Pawn, and he will experience certain difficulties in getting his Queen's Bishop into play, while White can push his King's Pawn at any time and thus free his Queen's Bishop.

(6) ...	B-K2
(7) N-R3	

(7) KN-B3, P-QN3; (8) N-K5, B-N2; (9) Q-B3, to prevent N-K5, is also a strong continuation.

(7) ...	P-QN3
(8) Castles	B-N2
(9) Q-B3	Q-B2
(10) N-B2	

A waiting move. The idea is to attack with P-KN4-N5 in case Black castles on the King's side, or with P-QR4-R5 in case he castles on the Queen's side. Furthermore, the move permits the Queen to leave her post without giving up control of K4.

(10) ...	B-Q3?

Intended to prevent P-K4, this move, in fact, encourages the advance of that Pawn. The loss of the King's Bishop's Pawn is more than compensated by the opening of the file in which White has his Queen and Rook. Castling on the Queen's side was probably Black's best plan.

(11) P-K4!	BxP?
(12) P-K5!	

Black should never have permitted this push. He should have exchanged the Pawn and castled on the King's side. As it is, Black is compelled to exchange his Bishop, and then to move the Knight which

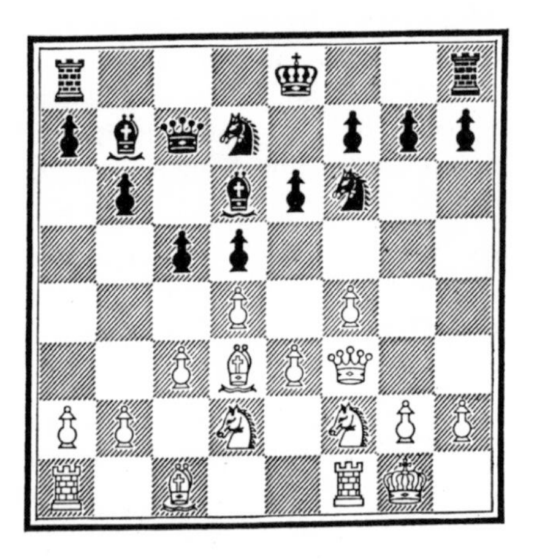

DIAGRAM 81

Position after the 10th move.

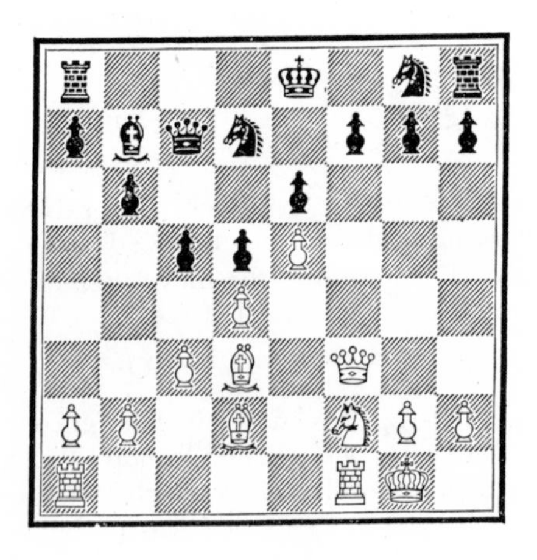

DIAGRAM 82

Position after the 13th move.

is attacked, leaving White with a dangerous initiative in the opened Bishop's file.

(12) ...	BxN
(13) BxB	N-KN1

N-K5 would have led to immediate disaster through (14) NxN, PxN; (15) QxPch, K-Q1; (16) QxNP, etc.

(14) N-K4!	NxP
(15) PxN	PxN
(16) BxP	BxB
(17) QxB	R-Q1

Apparently Black has eluded White's attack. He has succeeded in exchanging a good many pieces and maintained his extra-Pawn. However, his undeveloped King's wing gives White time to gather his remaining forces for a new onslaught.

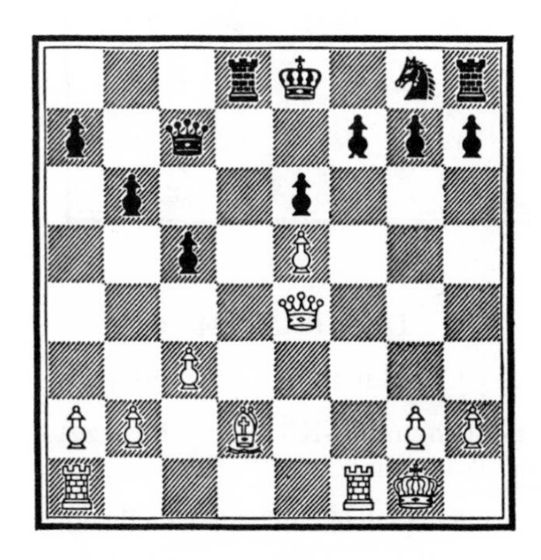

DIAGRAM 83

(18) Q-N4!	P-N3

Not QxP, because (19) B-B4, Q-B3; (20) B-B7 would win the exchange and several Pawns besides.

(19) B-N5	R-Q2

If N-K2 instead, (20) B-B6, Castles; (21) Q-R4, N-B4; (22) RxN, KPxR; (23) Q-R6 would be the end.

(20) QR-Q1	RxR
(21) RxR	N-K2

The coöperation of White's three attacking pieces now leads to a beautiful finish:

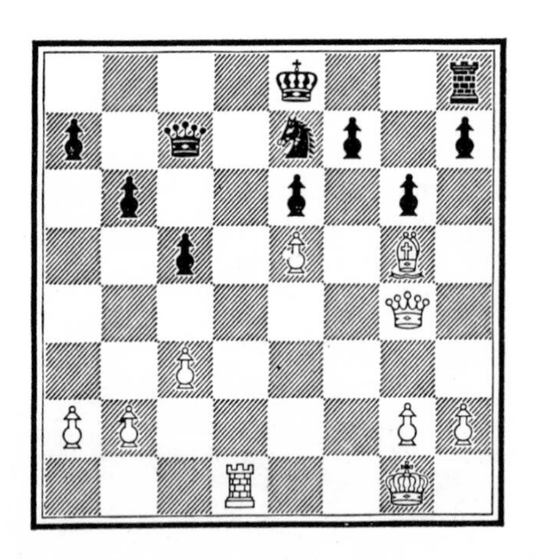

DIAGRAM 84

(22) Q-QR4ch	Q-B3

Or: K-B1; (23) B-R6ch and Q-K8 mate. Or: (22) . . ., N-B3; (23) QxNch!, QxQ; (24) R-Q8 mate.

(23) R-Q8ch!!	KxR
(24) QxQ	Resigns.

A very instructive example illustrating the dangers entailed in retarded development.

PART II

THE GAME OF CHECKERS

I

THE RULES OF THE GAME

The game of Checkers (English: Draughts) is played on the 32 black or white squares of the Chess board by two opponents, each of whom has twelve men of the same kind. The object of the game is to capture all opposing men or to block them so that they cannot move.

The original position of board and men is shown in Diagram 85. It will be seen that the board is placed in such a way that the players have a vacant square at their lower right hand corner. This corner is called the *double corner* because two men are located in its immediate neighborhood while the left hand corner, the *single corner*, is occupied by only one man.

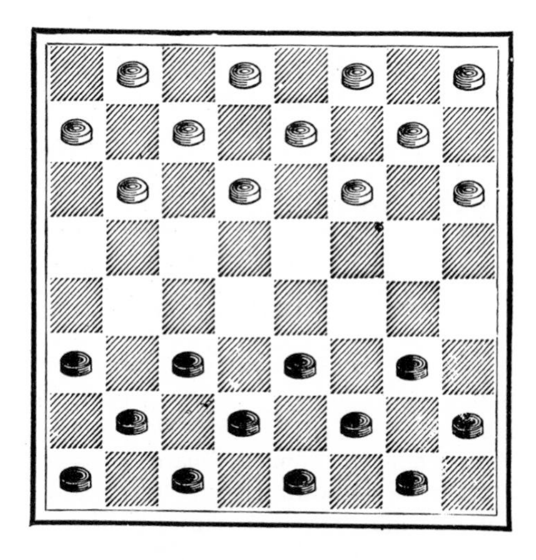

DIAGRAM 85

The squares of the Checker board are usually described by numbers as shown in Diagram 86. This is a rather crude method when compared with the simple notation by means of a system of coördinates as used in Chess, but as it is universally employed in Checker books and Checker columns in daily papers it will be adhered to in the following explanation of the game.

The black men are placed on the squares 1 to 12, the white men on the squares 21 to 32. The first move must invariably be made by the player of the black men.

The move of the Checker men is a diagonal step forward, one square at a time. If a hostile man is in his way and if the square beyond the

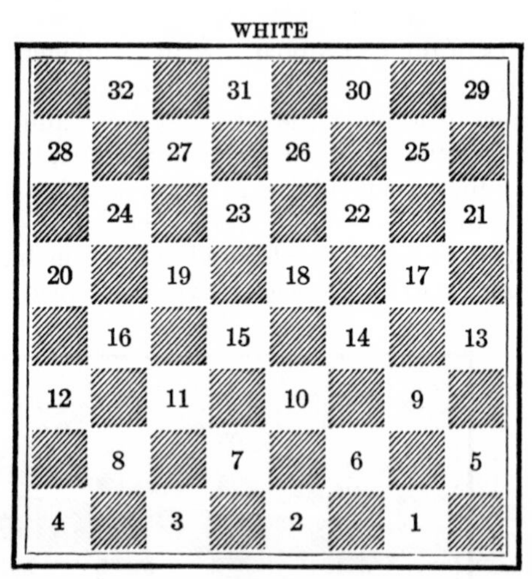

DIAGRAM 86

hostile man is vacant, he must capture him by jumping over him on to the vacant square, and he must continue capturing from the square on. which he lands as long as this is possible according to the above rule Captured men are removed from the board.

If a man reaches the opposite edge of the board he automatically becomes a King and must be "crowned" by the opponent, who must place another man on top of him. A King may move and capture backward as well as forward. A man, who reaches the "King row" in capturing, cannot, however, continue capturing on the same move with the newly made King.

The position of Diagram 87 may serve to illustrate the above rules. White, on the move, plays 14-9. Black must capture this man with the man on 5 who jumps on to 14. White then sacrifices another man by 23-18 forcing Black to reply 14-23. Now White captures the three men on 23, 15 and 7 with his man on 26, and Black, before making his next move, must crown White's man who has just reached the King's row. He will naturally move his man 8, as otherwise White would capture him with the King on 3.

If a player overlooks the possibility of a capture his opponent has the right to remove the man who should have made the capture, from the

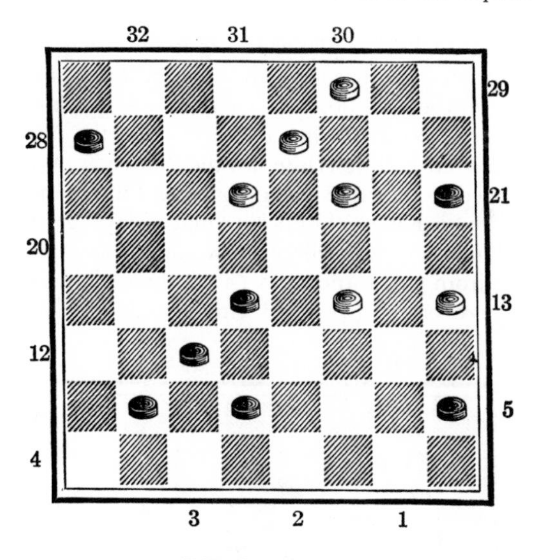

DIAGRAM 87

board. This procedure is called "huffing" and does not constitute a play. Instead of huffing a player may ask the opponent to retract his move and to make the capture.

When neither player can force a win the game is considered a draw. When one side appears to be stronger and refuses to accept a draw offered the player of the weaker side can require the win to be demonstrated within 40 moves; otherwise the game is drawn.

II

ELEMENTARY TACTICS

The first thing a Checker player has to know is what superiority in material or position is required to *force* a win in the ending. The most elementary case is the one shown in Diagram 88, in which White wins by playing 32-27. With this move White takes the opposition or as most Checker players call it, White has the "move." Whatever Black replies he is forced to the edge of the board and finally he is obliged to let White capture his King. Supposing Black plays (2) 26-22, in order to reach the double corner, where he would be safe as he could indefinitely move from 5 to 1 and from 1 to 5, then White continues with (2) . . ., 27-23, preventing (3) 22-18 which would gain the road to the

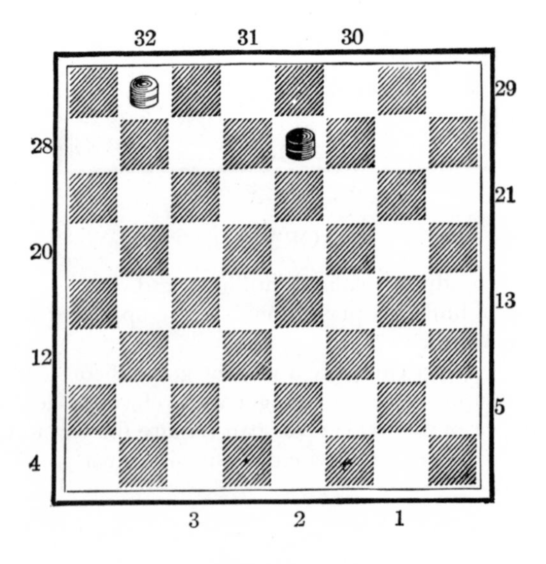

DIAGRAM 88

double corner. After (3) 22-17, 23-18; Black has to retreat to the edge by 17-13 or 17-21, and White, by playing 18-14, or 18-22 pins the black King so that he cannot move without being captured. If it had been Black's move in the position of the diagram, he would have gained the opposition by 26-31 and White would have been compelled to retire to the double corner and to draw by 32-28, 28-32, etc.

With one King entrenched in the double corner it takes two Kings to force the win. In the position of Diagram 89 for instance White would win as follows:

	Black	White
(1)	...	19-24
(2)	32-28	23-19
(3)	28-32	24-28
(4)	32-27	28-32
(5)	27-31	19-15
(6)	31-26	15-18
(7)	26-31	18-22

In the ending *Three Kings against two Kings* the most favorable spots for the weaker player are the two double corners; but the three Kings

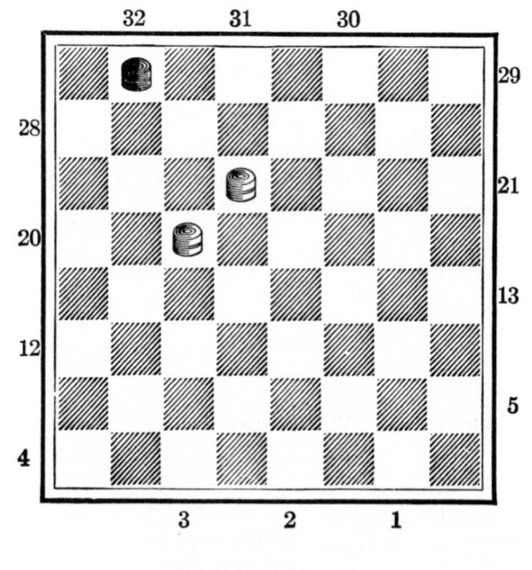

DIAGRAM 89

will always win when handled right. The method which has to be employed will be evident from the play in Diagram 90. In order to win Black must exchange one King; the position is then reduced to that of Diagram 89. If it were White's move, Black would easily win; for

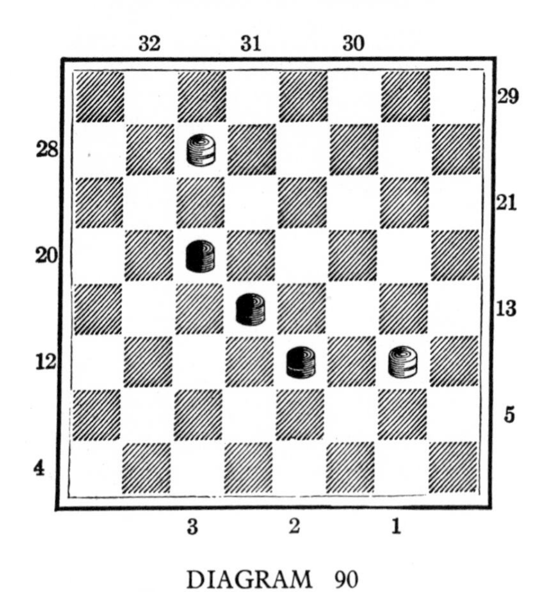

DIAGRAM 90

after (1) . . ., 27-32; (2) 19-24, 9-5; (3) 10-6, White cannot avoid the exchange. For instance: (3) . . ., 5-1; (4) 24-19. The problem reduces itself therefore to changing the move from Black to White. This is accomplished by:

Black	White
(1) 15-18	27-32
(2) 19-24	9-5
(3) 10-14	

Threatening 24-27. White can only reply

(3) . . .	32-28
(4) 24-27	5-1
(5) 14-9, etc., as above.	

If the weaker side does not control both double corners the exchange can be forced much more easily, as an experiment will quickly show. Sometimes the stronger side has an occasion to give up two Kings for one thereby forcing a position similar to that of Diagram 88. Diagram 91 offers an example:

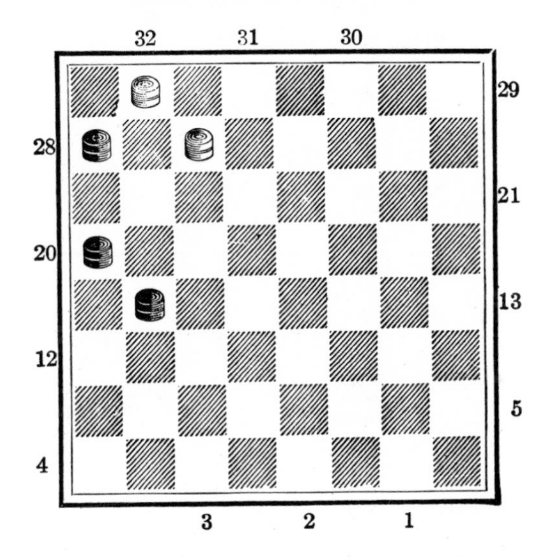

DIAGRAM 91

Black on the move wins in 5 moves, thus:

(1) 16-19 — 27-31
(2) 20-24 — 32-27
(3) 28-32 — 27x20
(4) 19-24 — 20x27
(5) 32x23

and White is pinned.

With three Kings against four a player can sometimes offer prolonged resistance. But finally the stronger player will always be able to force an exchange which secures the victory. In the position of Diagram 92 for instance Black will proceed as follows:

(1) 18-15 — 19-24

It would not help to play 27-24, as Black would reply 14-17 and exchange on the next move by 10-14.

(2) 11-16

limiting White's mobility.

(2) . . . — 23-26

In answer to 24-20 Black would play 15-19.

(3)	16-19	24-28
(4)	14-18	26-30
(5)	19-23	28-32
(6)	15-19	27-31

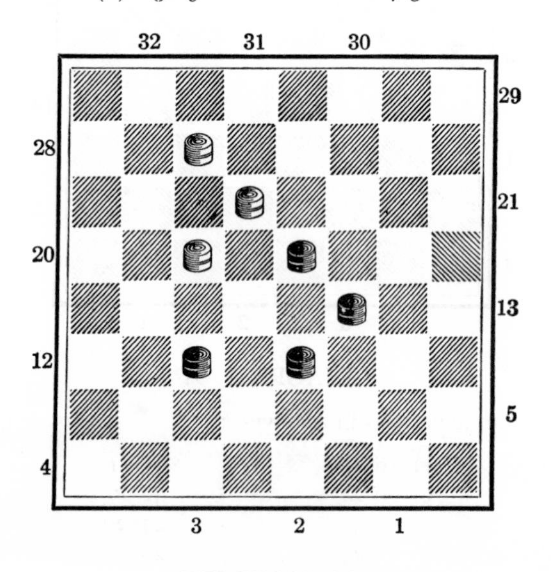

DIAGRAM 92

Not 30-25 on account of 18-22.

(7)	10-14	31-26
(8)	14-17	26-31
(9)	17-22	31-27
(10)	19-16	27-24
(11)	16-19 and wins.	

If, on the 10th move, White played 27-31 instead of 27-24, the game might proceed as follows:

(11)	18-15	32-28
(12)	15-19	28-32
(13)	22-26	31x22

(14)	23-27	32x23
(15)	19x17	

These possibilities of exchanging "two for two" should always be looked for as they often occur, enabling a win within a few moves.

III

THE FIVE FUNDAMENTAL POSITIONS

While in the examples of elementary endings given in the previous chapter, the correct method of play was comparatively easy to find, positions with few men often occur which look very simple but which require considerable thought to be handled in the right way. The knowledge of these positions, of which there are five distinctly different types, is essential for any one who desires to become a fair player and they are, therefore, thoroughly explained in the following five characteristic examples.

THE FIRST POSITION

It does not make any difference in the method of play whether the

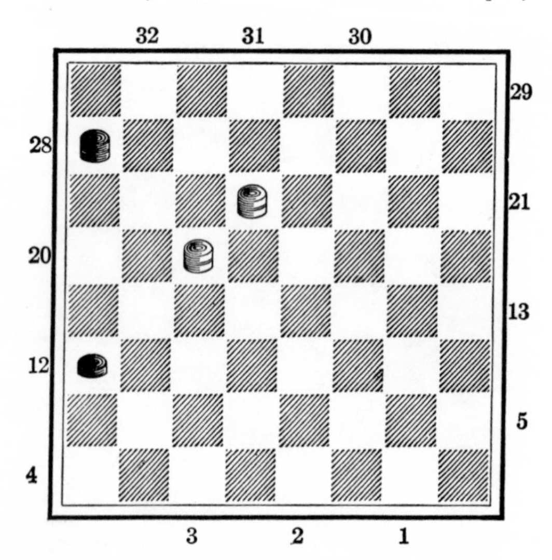

DIAGRAM 93—WHITE TO MOVE AND WIN

Black man is located as shown in Diagram 93 or on 3, 4, 7, 8, 10, 11, 16, 20 or 24. The essential point is that he must not be able to march to the King row without being intercepted by White.

The winning maneuver is this: White turns the Black King out of the double corner in the manner shown in the play from the position of Diagram 89 and thereby compels the Black man to advance, finally forcing an exchange which secures the opposition. This maneuver, as will be evident from a careful study of the position, is possible only in case White has the move. If Black has the move the ending is a draw.

Black	White
(1) . . .	23-27
(2) 28-32	19-23
(3) 32-28	

Black cannot play 12-16, as 27-24 would win a piece.

(3) . . .	27-32
(4) 28-24	

Again 12-16 is not possible on account of 32-27 winning a piece in three moves.

(4) . . .	23-18

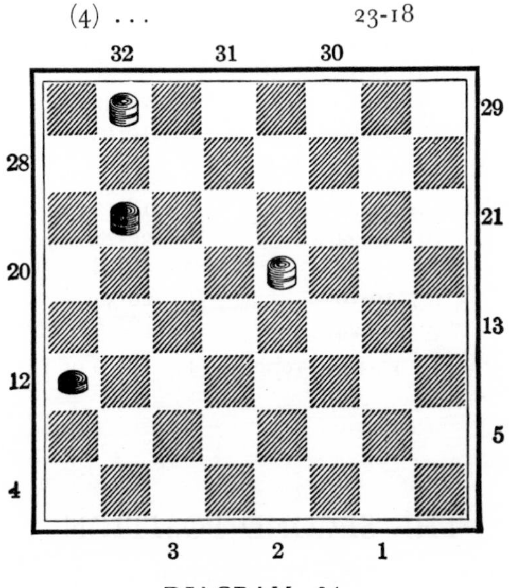

DIAGRAM 94

If White played 32-28 Black would exchange by (5) 24-19 and draw the game.

In the position of the Diagram Black has the choice between 24-20, 12-16, 24-19 or 24-28, but he loses, no matter what move he makes as demonstrated below.

(A)	(5)	24-20	32-27
	(6)	20-16	18-15
	(7)	16-20	15-18
	(8)	12-16	18-15
(B)	(5)	12-16	18-15

Now Black cannot play (6) 16-19 because of the exchange 32-27; (6) 16-20 would also lose quickly through 15-18, (7) 24-19, 32-28, (8) 19-16, 18-23. The best try is (6) 24-28.

Against 15-18 Black would now draw by (7) 16-19, 32-27; (8) 19-23. The only way to win is

(6)	...	15-11

after which Black can do no better than

	(7)	16-19	32-27
	(8)	28-32	27-31
	(9)	32-28	11-16
	(10)	19-24	16-19, etc.
(C)	(5)	24-19	32-28
	(6)	12-16	28-32
	(7)	19-24	18-15

and White continues as shown before.

(D)	(5)	24-28	18-15
	(6)	28-24	32-28
	(7)	24-27	15-18
	(8)	12-16	28-32
	(9)	27-24	18-15

and wins as before by 15-18 in reply to (10) 16-20 or 15-11 in reply to 24-28.

THE SECOND POSITION

(See Diagram 95)

White's advantage is that he can crown his two men while Black remains with only one King and two men. The reason why Black cannot use his two men to advantage is that they are pinned on the side of the board while White's men are located in the center where they have much more mobility. All the same White must have the move in order to win, just as in first position.

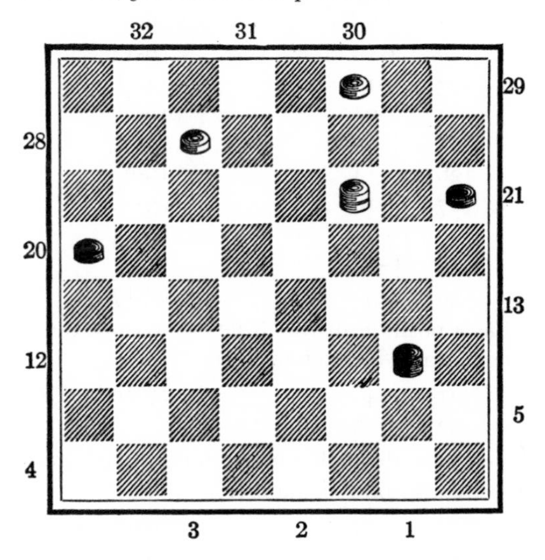

DIAGRAM 95—WHITE TO MOVE AND WIN

	Black	White
(1)	. . .	30-26
(2)	9-14	26-23
(3)	14-10	23-18
(4)	10-6	18-14
(5)	6-1	14-9
(6)	1-5	9-6
(7)	5-9	6-2
(8)	9-5	2-6
(9)	5-1	6-9
(10)	1-5	9-14
(11)	5-1	14-18
(12)	1-6	18-15
(13)	6-9	15-19
(14)	9-14	27-23
(15)	14-10	23-18

(16)	10-6	18-14
(17)	6-1	14-9
(18)	1-5	9-6
(19)	5-9	6-2
(20)	9-5	2-6
(21)	5-1	6-9
(22)	1-5	9-14
(23)	5-1	14-18
(24)	1-6	18-23
(25)	6-10	23-27
(26)	10-14	19-23
(27)	14-10	23-18
(28)	10-6	18-14
(29)	6-1	14-9
(30)	1-5	22-17

At last White has a position in which he can reduce the ending to one of the fundamental cases by exchange.

(31)	5-14	17-10
(32)	21-25	

It will be noticed that through the exchange Black gained to move. White regains it by a second exchange.

(32)	...	10-15
(33)	25-30	15-19
(34)	30-26	27-32
(35)	26-22	19-24
(36)	20-27	32-23

and wins.

Second position as a rule results from a "Bridge position" like the following: Black men on 20, 21, 23, Black King on 26. White men on 30 and 32, White Kings on 15 and 19. Black to move:

(1)	26-31	19-26
(2)	31-22	32-27

and White wins by "second position."

THE CHANGE OF THE MOVE

By the exchanges of men in the foregoing example the move was altered in each case. However, exchanges of pieces often occur which do *not* change the move, and as win or loss in a great number of endings depends upon which player has the move, it is necessary for the beginner to obtain a clear insight into the questions involved. An exchange always alters the move if the capturing piece is recaptured in turn. If

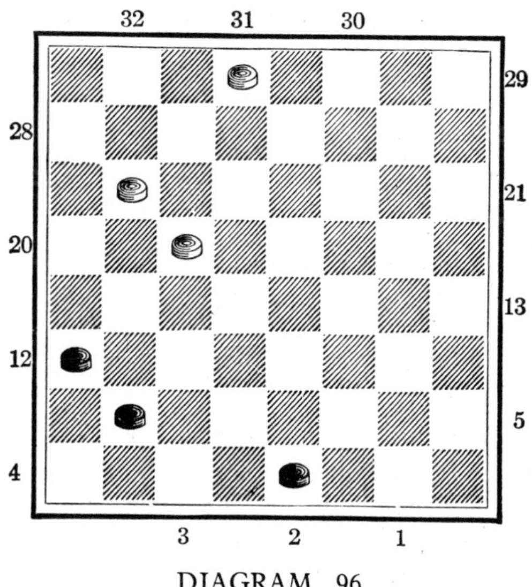

DIAGRAM 96

a different piece is recaptured, it depends upon the relative position of the captured pieces, whether the move has remained with the same player or gone over to his opponent. For the purpose of calculating the move and its changes it is useful to imagine the Checker board as being composed of two "systems of squares"—the Black system containing the ranks starting with the squares 1, 9, 17 and 25, and the White system containing the other four ranks. If each of the two systems contains an *even* number of men, the player whose turn to play it is, loses the opposition, that is: his opponent has the move. If the number of men in each system is *odd*, the player whose turn to play it is, gains the opposition, that is, he has the move. As the calculation of the move enters only into such positions in which both players have the same number of pieces, it is sufficient to count the number of men in one of the systems to obtain the desired information. Diagram 96 furnishes an example.

Counting the men of a system, the Black one, for instance, shows their number to be odd. Therefore, the player whose turn it is to play has the move, which in the present instance secures the win for White and a draw for Black, thus

(A) Black to move

Black	White
(1) 8-11	

This is apparently Black's best move; if he plays 2-7, White replies 19-15, obtaining a very strong position.

(1) . . .	31-26
(2) 2-6	26-22
(3) 6-10	22-18
(4) 11-16	18-15

Draw.

(B) White to move

Black	White
(1) . . .	31-26
(2) 2-6	26-22
(3) 8-11	24-20
(4) 6-10	22-19

Block.

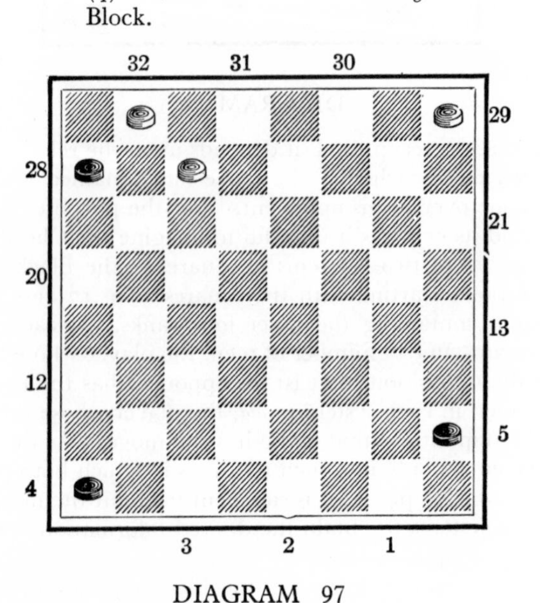

DIAGRAM 97

From the above explanation it is evident that in the case of an exchange the move remains unaltered if the captured pieces were located in the same system, and that the move changes if the captured pieces belonged to different systems.

Exceptions to the rule sometimes occur due to a piece having no mobility, as for instance in the position of Diagram 97 where Black, on the move, loses because his man on 28 is blocked.

THE THIRD POSITION

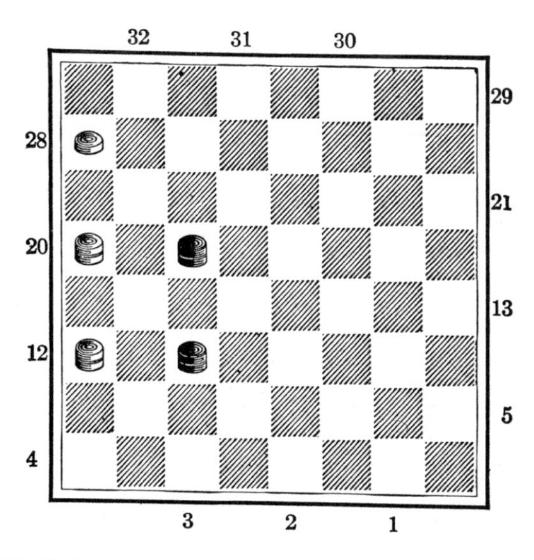

DIAGRAM 98—WHITE TO MOVE AND WIN

White being a man ahead appears to have an easy win; but owing to the difficulty of getting the man crowned he has a hard task before him.

If the Kings on 11 and 12 were removed White would not be able to win at all, as the Black King would go back and forth between 19 and 23. It is, therefore, clear that in forcing a win from the position of the diagram the King on 12 must coöperate.

Another point to be borne in mind is that the following position would be a draw with White to move.

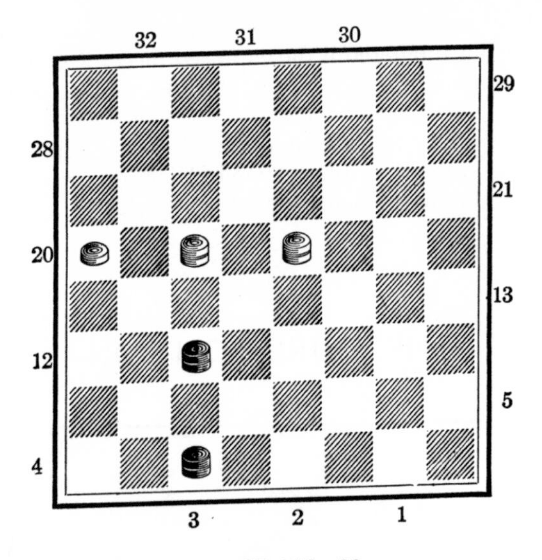

DIAGRAM 99

White is unable to make any headway because he cannot threaten an exchange. The method in which White threatens the exchange of the King on 19 in the example of third position given in Diagram 98 is the following:

Black	White
(1) . . .	20-24
(2) 11-15	24-27

12-8 would be of no use as 19-23 would force 8-12 again.

(3) 15-11	

If 15-18 White wins by 27-31

(3) . . .	27-32

27-31 would admit of a draw by (4) 19-23, 28-24; (5) 23-27, 24-20; (6) 27-23, 12-16; (7) 11-15, etc.

(4) 11-15	12-8
(5) 15-18	32-27
(6) 18-15	27-31
(7) 15-18	8-11
(8) 18-23	11-7

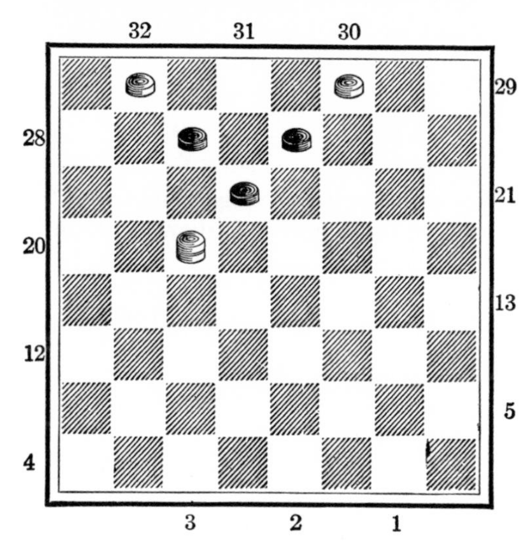

DIAGRAM 100

(9) 19-15

This is better than allowing the Kings to get together.

(9)	. . .	28-24
(10)	23-27	24-20
(11)	27-23	7-2
(12)	15-11	2-6
(13)	23-19	6-10

If he moved the other King, Black would draw by 19-16.

(14)	19-23	10-14
(15)	23-19	

Black would lose easily if he allowed the man to advance

(15) . . . 14-18

Threatening to exchange

(16) 19-24

The only move to avoid the exchange.

(16)	. . .	18-23
(17)	24-28	23-19

(18)	28-32	31-26
(19)	32-28	26-23
(20)	28-32	23-18
(21)	32-28	19-15
(22)	11-8	20-16

and White cannot be prevented from getting another King.

An earlier setting of third position is shown in Diagram 100.

White wins by

(1)	. . .	19-24
(2)	27-31	32-28
(3)	23-27	30-23
(4)	27-32	23-18
(5)	32-27	24-20
(6)	27-23	19-15, etc.

THE FOURTH POSITION

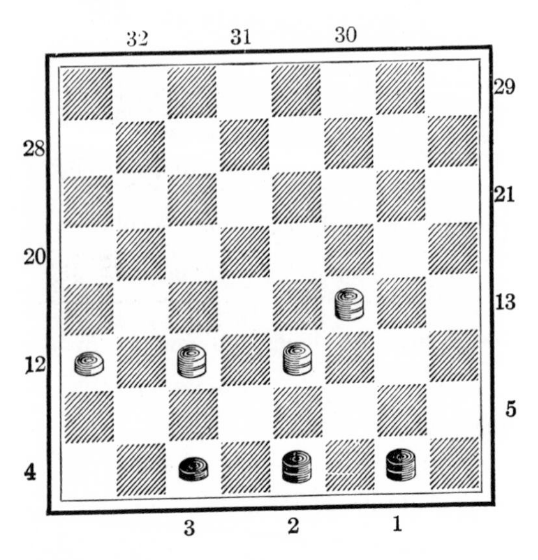

DIAGRAM 101—WHITE TO MOVE AND WIN

Although White is a piece ahead he has great difficulties in winning on account of the weak position of the man on 12. Black's man on 3 holds him in check without being impaired in his effectiveness towards the center of the board. If Black had the move, White could not win at all, as he would be unable to dislodge Black's Kings. As it is, he wins by means of a sacrifice which often occurs in endings with 4 Kings against 3.

Black	White
(1) . . .	14-9
(2) 1-5	9-13
(3) 5-1	11-15
(4) 2-6	10-14
(5) 1-5	15-18
(6) 5-1	

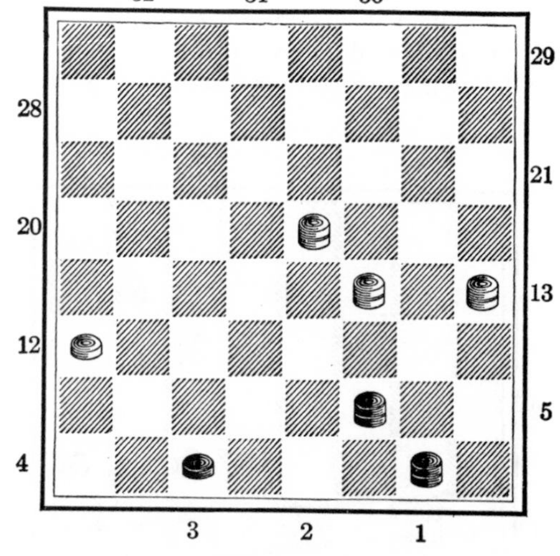

DIAGRAM 102

It would not help Black to play 6-2 on account of 13-9; (7) 5-1, 9-5; (8) 2-6, 14-17; (9) 6-2, 17-13; (10) 2-6, 18-15; (11) 6-2, 15-10, etc.

(6) . . .	14-9
(7) 6-2	9-5
(8) 2-6	18-15
(9) 6-2	15-10

This is the important move, which forces the win.

(10) 2-6

If 2-7, White exchanges by 13-9

(10) . . . 10-7

Only with this pretty sacrifice can White win the game. After (11) 3-10 White plays 5-9 and should Black answer (12) 6-2, White would get "two for one" by 9-6. Therefore, Black can do no better than play (12) 10-15, 9-2; (13) 15-19, etc., and get a King in each double corner. White then wins as explained in the chapter on elementary endings.

Fourth position results in a draw only when the man is held on 12 or 21, according to whether the weaker side is Black or White. In third position it is useless to hold the man on the above squares, but sometimes a draw is obtained by holding him on 20 or 13.

In defending a game with two Kings against two Kings and a man, the weaker side must have the move in the system in which the man is pinned. The following position for instance is drawn with White on the move.

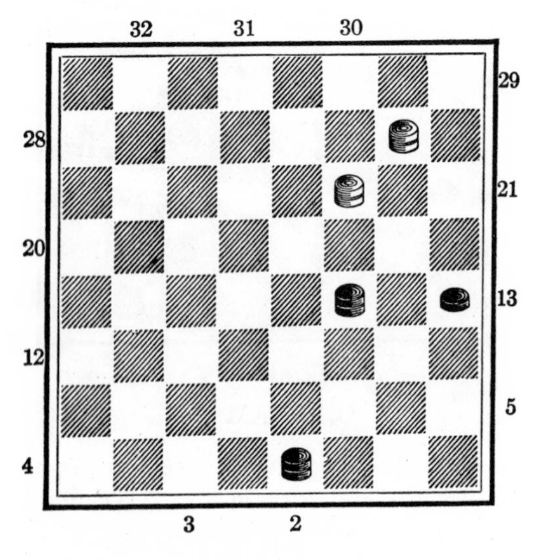

DIAGRAM 103

Black, on the move, would win by (1) 13-17, 22-13; (2) 14-9.

In Diagram 104 the drawing move is 27-31. The game ought to run like this:

(2)	20-24	23-27
(3)	24-28	27-32
(4)	30-26	31-27
(5)	22-18	27-24
(6)	26-23	24-20

and White moves back and forth between 24 and 20.

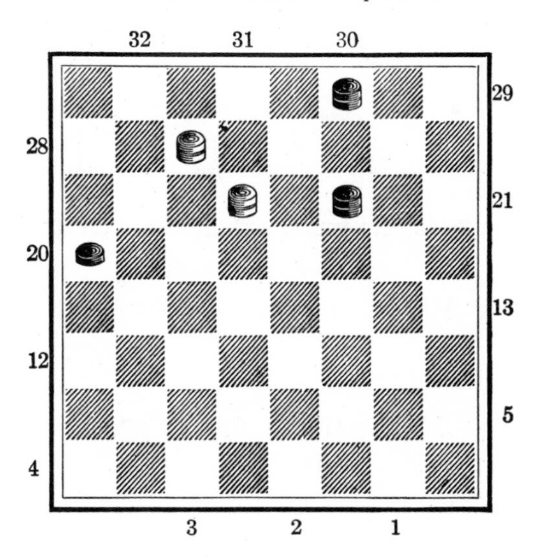

DIAGRAM 104—WHITE TO MOVE

In the position of Diagram 105 White draws by:

(1)	. . .	23-19
(2)	28-32	19-24
(3)	7-2	24-19
(4)	2-6	19-24
(5)	6-9	24-19
(6)	9-14	19-24
(7)	14-17	15-19

Changing the guard

(8)	17-22	19-23

and Black can make no progress.

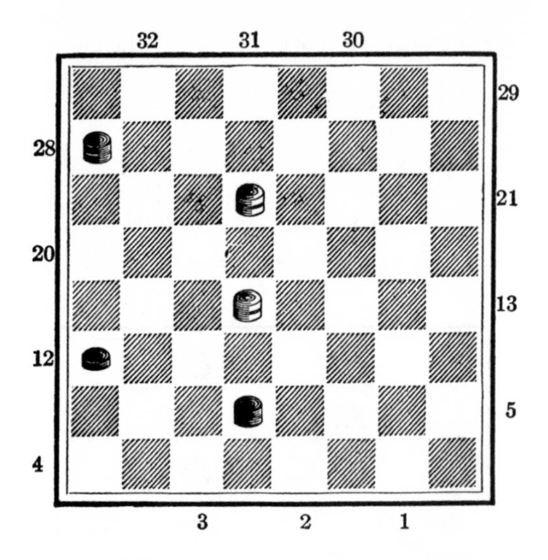

DIAGRAM 105—WHITE TO MOVE

THE FIFTH POSITION

See Diagram 106.

White is on the move, and it is evident that he loses if he moves the man on 27 permitting black to reply 11-15. The only way to save the game is to sacrifice the man on 20 by 20-16. The following play would ensue.

(2)	11-20	27-23
(3)	20-24	22-18
(4)	24-27	18-9
(5)	10-14	

Preventing 23-18

(5)	. . .	9-6
(6)	27-31	6-2K
(7)	31-27	2-6

White cannot save the piece and so he runs his opponent.

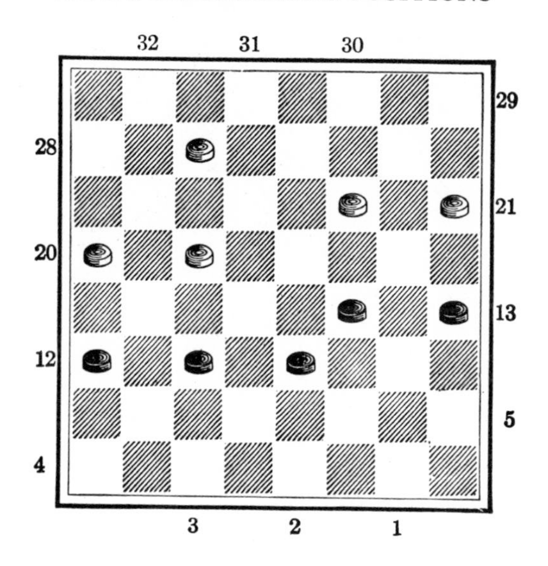

DIAGRAM 106

(8)	27-18	6-9
(9)	13-17	19-15
(10)	18-11	9-18
(11)	17-22	18-25
(12)	11-15	25-22

Drawn. White would lose by 21-17, as after (13) 15-18, 17-13; (14) 18-14, 25-22; (15) 12-16 he cannot gain the double corner.

The following has been suggested as a suitable problem to be called *Sixth Position. (See Diagram 107.)*

Black plays

(1) 7-2

threatening (2) 3-7 and (3) 15-11. White can prevent this only by

(1) . . . 24-20

Now 3-7 would only draw on account of 16-11.

(2)	2-6	20-24
(3)	6-10	24-20

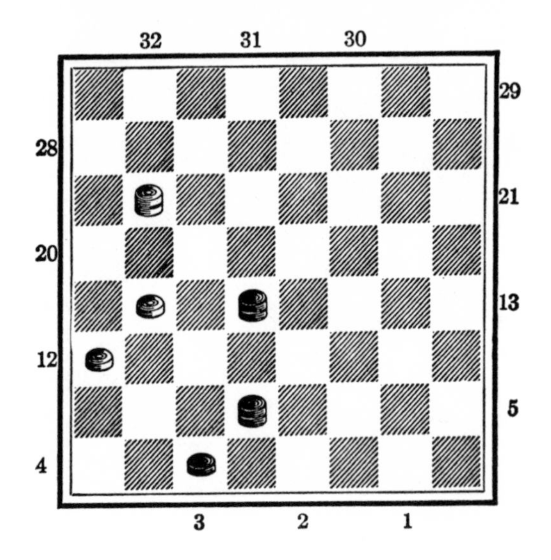

DIAGRAM 107—BLACK TO MOVE AND WHITE TO DRAW

Again 3-7 had to be prevented.

(4)	10-14	20-24
(5)	14-17	24-27

This time 24-20 would have lost, as Black would have replied (6) 17-13, 20-24; (7) 3-7, 12-8; (8) 15-11.

(6)	17-13	27-32

Avoiding 27-24 which would lose by (7) 3-7

(7)	13-9	32-27
(8)	9-14	27-24
(9)	14-18	24-27

Drawn. White has to watch 3-7 and to take care to play 24-20 at the right time so as to exchange 16-11 if 3-7 is played. At the same time he must beware of playing 24-20 when the Black Kings are on squares 15 and 5 or 15 and 13, as otherwise Black would reply 5-9, 20-24; 3-7, 12-8; 15-11.

IV

GENERAL PRINCIPLES AND ILLUSTRATIVE GAMES

It is possible to apply general strategic principles to the game of Checkers, just as well as the game of Chess, even though there is not the scope in Checkers for strategic maneuvers on the grand scale on which they can be carried out in Chess.

Again it is naturally the principle of greatest mobility which should govern the plan of mobilization in any opening, and it is consequently more desirable to have the men work in the center of the board, than on the edge, where part of their range is cut off.

The advantage of center squares over side squares is not so marked in Checkers as it is in Chess. There is no doubt that a piece has more mobility in the center, where there are two or four moves to choose from, than on the side where only one or two moves are possible; but a man on the side has an advantage in so far as he is backed up by the edge of the board so that he is safe from being captured until he moves. However, a player who keeps his men in massed formation in the center will in almost all cases be able to make them protect each other and to win the upper hand against an opponent whose army is divided into two parts, one on the left and the other on the right side of the board.

When playing with the white men, it is advisable to occupy such squares as 14, 18, 19, 30, 31 and 32, and it is not advisable to occupy 5 and 12 whenever the opponent has a man on 1 or 3 respectively, as in that case the men have a tendency to act as supports for the enemy instead of helping their own side. In the position: Black 1, 7 and 9; White 5, 14, 18 and 22; for instance, White's man on 5 supports Black's man on 9 and White, on the move, has to surrender a piece by 22-17, to which Black replies 9-13.

It is naturally a good thing not to touch the men of the back row mentioned above, as they will prevent the opponent from getting Kings. White's man 29 and Black's man 4, however, are better off in the middle of the board, as the squares 25 and 8 are adequately guarded by 30 and 3 respectively. Moreover, there is danger of the first position arising from openings in which a player keeps his man in the single corner.

A formation which very often occurs in the middle game is the so-called "elbow." It consists of three men arranged like the white pieces in Diagram 108.

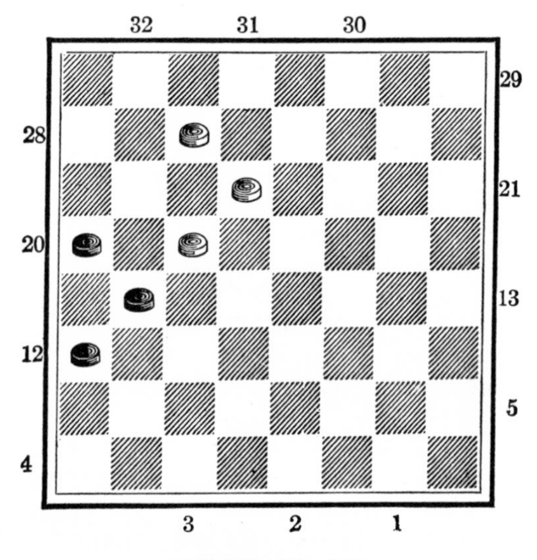

DIAGRAM 108

When adequately supported an elbow forms a solid position which cannot easily be attacked. An example of a strong elbow will be found in the following game:

	Black	White
(1)	10-15	23-19
(2)	6-10	22-17
(3)	1-6	25-22
(4)	11-16	17-13
(5)	16-23	26-19
(6)	7-11	29-25
(7)	11-16	22-17
(8)	16-23	27-11
(9)	8-15	24-19
(10)	15-24	28-19
(11)	4-8	25-22
(12)	8-11	31-26
(13)	3-7	22-18

(14) 9-14	18-9
(15) 5-14	

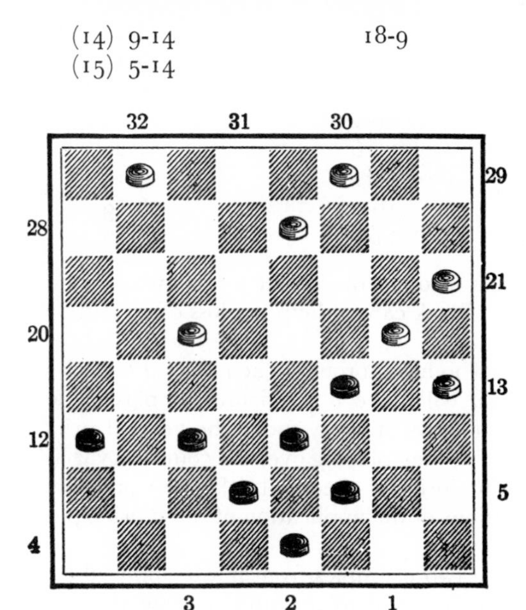

DIAGRAM 109

The men on 6, 10, 13, 14, 17 and 21 form the elbow, the strength of which becomes apparent on the 19th move.

(15) . . .	26-23
(16) 11-15	32-28
(17) 15-24	28-19
(18) 7-11	30-26
(19) 2-7	19-16
(20) 12-19	23-16
(21) 11-20	26-23
(22) 7-11 and wins.	

The danger involved in an elbow, which is not sufficiently backed up, is shown in the following game.

Black	White
(1) 10-15	23-19
(2) 7-10	22-17
(3) 3-7	25-22
(4) 9-14	29-25

(5) 5-9	17-13
(6) 1-5	22-17
(7) 11-16	26-22
(8) 16-23	27-11
(9) 7-16	31-26
(10) 8-11	24-19
(11) 16-23	26-19
(12) 11-15	30-26

and White wins through the threat to get two for one by 19-15 after the exchange. Black cannot help the loss of a man.

The reader, who has thoroughly acquainted himself with the fundamental endings, will have no difficulty in playing a good game of checkers, if he follows at every move the general principles discussed in this chapter. When playing over the countless variations, which are offered in the majority of checker books, he would find that they are merely illustrations of the application of those principles to the various openings.

Following are two examples from master play, the careful study of which will do more good to the student than the perusal of a great number of games that lack adequate annotation.

Black	White
(1) 9-14	

The best opening move is probably 11-15, as this enables a speedy development of the man on 4, who, as previously explained, should not be kept in the back row. The variations resulting from 11-15 have been so thoroughly analyzed that it is practically impossible to defeat a player who chooses this opening and knows the possible variations by heart. It has, therefore, been found necessary to restrict the players in matches and tournaments by balloting the first move of Black and White, in order to avoid too many draws. This is a serious drawback as it curtails the freedom of decision to which a player should be entitled in any game.

(1) . . .	22-17
(2) 11-15	

It is hard to tell whether this move or 11-16 or 5-9 is the best. 6-9 and 10-15 are considered weak.

(2) . . .	25-22

More aggressive than 23-19, which can safely be played.

(3) 15-19

8-11 or 17-13 or 23-19 are also good moves.

(3) ...	24-15
(4) 10-19	23-16
(5) 12-19	17-10
(6) 6-15	21-17
(7) 5-9	29-25
(8) 8-12	25-21
(9) 7-10	17-13

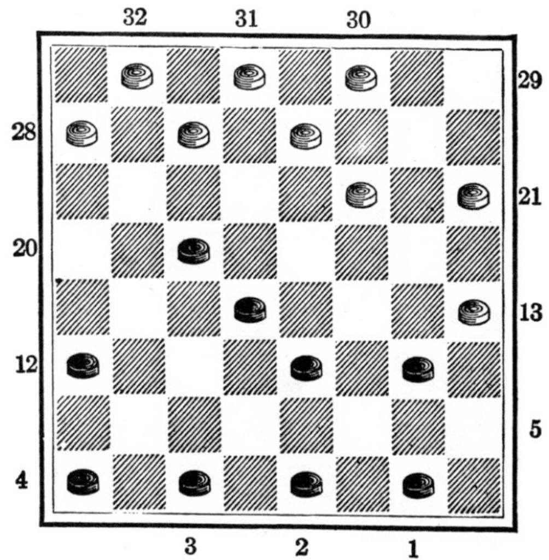

DIAGRAM 110

(10) 1-6

At first sight, it might seem unwise to break up the King row, when 9-14 could be played; but the advantage of holding the man on 13, instead of allowing him to complicate matters by 13-9, more than counterbalances the disadvantage of moving a back man. Black could also play (10) 2-6, but this admits of the following strong attack: (10) 2-6, 27-23; (11) 4-8, 23-16; (12) 12-19, 32-27; (13) 9-14, 27-24; (14) 3-7 (8-12 would lose), 22-17; (15) 14-18 (again 8-12 would lose), 17-14; (16) 10-17, 21-14; (17) 1-5, 31-27; (18) 6-10, 24-20; (19) 10-17, 26-22;

(20) 18-25, 30-14; (21) 7-11 (Probably the only move to draw—8-12 would lose on account of 20-16).

(10) . . . 27-24
(11) 4-8 32-27

22-18 could also be played.

(12) 9-14 27-23

or 22-17 or 24-20.

(13) 3-7 23-16
(14) 12-19 22-17
(15) 7-11 26-23

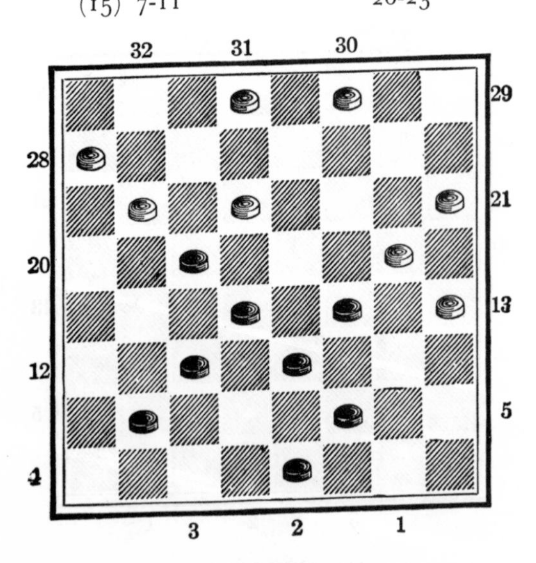

DIAGRAM 111

31-27 would lose through (16) 8-12, 26-22; (17) 11-16, 24-20; (18) 19-24, 20-11; (19) 24-31, 11-8; (20) 14-18.

(16) 19-26 30-23
(17) 8-12 24-20
(18) 15-18 23-19

20-16 cannot be played on account of (19) 20-27, 16-7; (20) 2-11, 31-24; (21) 12-16.

(19) 11-15 20-16

White can, of course, draw here by 31-26; but 20-16 also draws in spite of Black's seemingly invincible elbow.

(20) 15-24	28-19
(21) 2-7	31-26
(22) 18-23	

If 18-22, White draws by 19-15; (23) 12-19, 13-9.

(22) . . .	26-22

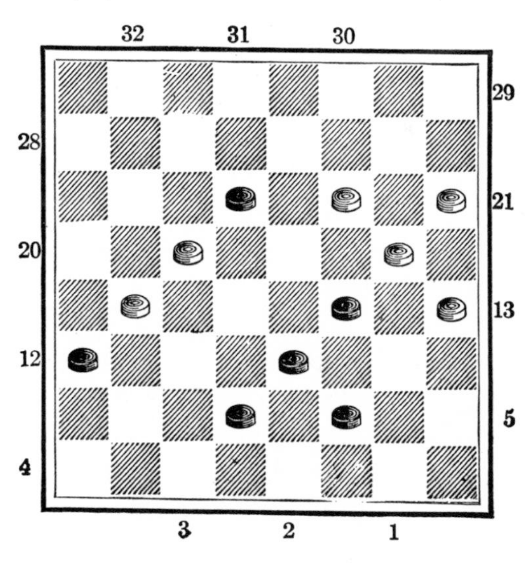

DIAGRAM 112

Playing for a brilliant finish. He could also draw by 16-11; (23) 7-16, 26-22; (24) 14-18, 22-15; (25) 23-26, 17-14.

(23) 23-27	16-11
(24) 7-23	22-18

Drawing, although two men down.

The following game illustrates first position:

Black	White
(1) 11-15	22-18

This move is not considered as strong as 23-19.

(2) 15-22	25-18
(3) 8-11	

12-16 can also be played.

(3) . . .	29-25
(4) 4-8	25-22

24-20 is another good move.

(5) 12-16

If 10-15, White obtains a strong game by 23-19.

(5) . . .	24-20

Considered best. 24-19 or 22-17 are also playable.

(6) 8-12

He could lay a trap by (6) 10-15. If White replies 27-24 or 28-24, Black wins by (7) 15-19, 24-15; (8) 16-19, 23-16; (9) 9-14.

(6) . . .	27-24
(7) 10-14	24-19

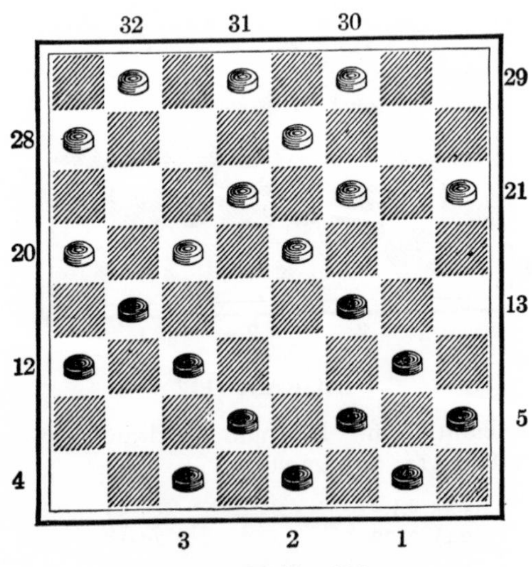

DIAGRAM 113

In answer to 31-27, Black would win by (8) 7-10, 24-19; (9) 9-13, 18-9; (10) 5-14, 28-24; (11) 13-17, 22-13; (12) 3-7 or (10) . . ., 27-24; (11) 1-5, 22-18; (12) 3-7.

(8) 7-10	28-24

32-27 or 19-15 are considered stronger.

(9) 3-7	32-28

This loses. The only drawing move is 30-25.

(10) 9-13	18-9
(11) 5-14	22-18

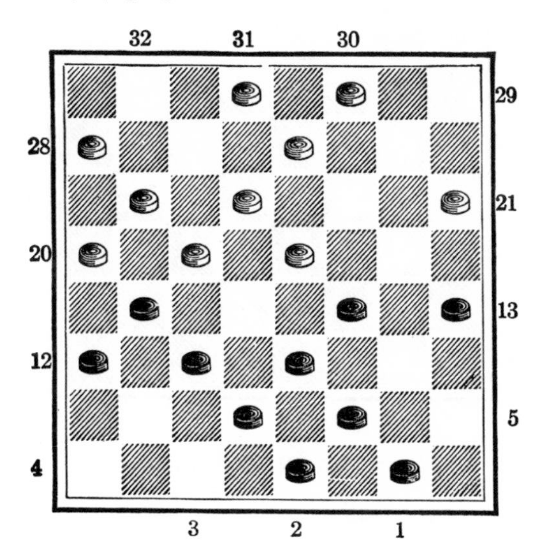

DIAGRAM 114

Four variations are possible here. If 31-27 or 30-25, Black wins by (12) 13-17, 22-13; (13) 14-18, etc. (11) . . ., 22-17 loses on account of (12) 13-22, 26-17; (13) 14-18. The sacrifice (11) . . ., 21-17; (12) 14-21, 22-18 is met by (13) 10-14, 18-9; (14) 1-5, 26-22; (15) 5-14, 31-26; (16) 13-17.

(12) 13-17	18-9
(13) 6-13	21-14
(14) 10-17	26-22

In answer to 30-25 Black wins by (15) 7-10, 25-22; (16) 2-6; but with 31-27 White can offer prolonged resistance, thus:
(14) . . ., 31-27; (15) 17-22, 26-17; (16) 13-22, 19-15; (17) 11-18, 23-14; (18) 1-6, 20-11; (19) 7-16, 27-23; (20) 16-19, 23-16; (21) 12-19, 24-15; (22) 6-10, 15-6; (23) 2-18, 28-24; (24) 18-23, 24-19; (25) 23-27, 19-15; (26) 27-32, 15-10; (27) 32-27, 10-6; (28) 27-23, 6-1; (29) 22-26, 1-6; (30) 26-31, 6-9; (31) 30-26, 9-13; (32) 26-22, 13-9; (33) 23-18. Black has now received first position and wins.

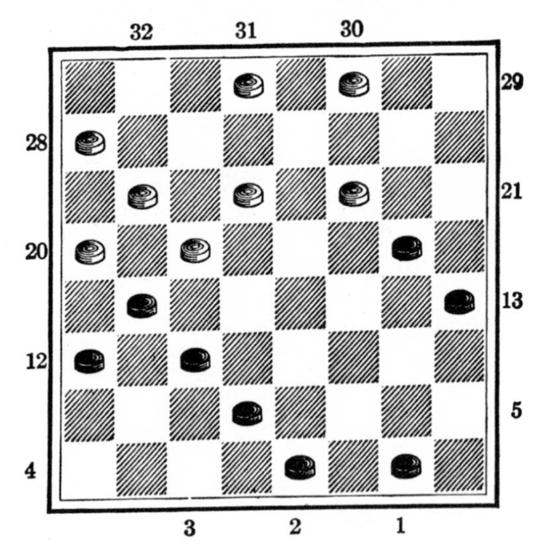

DIAGRAM 115

(15) 17-26 31-22
(16) 7-10 30-25
(17) 2-6 25-21
(18) 6-9 22-18
(19) 1-5 18-15

White must give up a piece to get through, and Black can then exchange at his leisure and win without difficulty.

(20) 11-27, etc.

V

PROBLEMS

Checker problems, unlike the Chess problems, are intimately related to the game itself and do not enable combinations different in kind from those which occur in the actual fight over the board. They usually represent an end game and are distinguished from ordinary endings only by an unexpected initial move, mostly embodying a sacrifice of several men. Diagrams 116, 117 and 118 furnish some examples:

PROBLEM No. 1 WHITE—TO MOVE AND DRAW

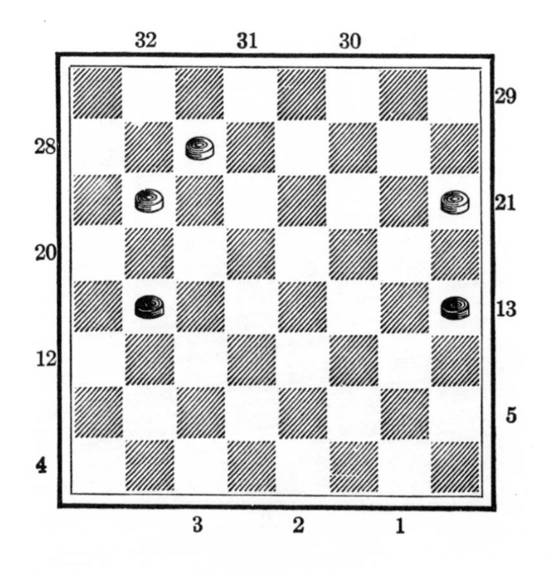

DIAGRAM 116

If, in Diagram 116, White tried to reach the King row with his man 27, Black would win by first position thus: (1) . . ., 27-23; (2) 16-20, 24-19; (3) 20-24, 19-15; (4) 24-27, 23-19; (5) 27-24, 19-16; (6)24-19, etc. The only way to draw is to sacrifice first the man on 21 by 21-17; and then to continue as above. This enables White to play 23-18, instead of 19-15, exchanging the King for a man.

The first move in Diagram 117 is 24-28, to which Black must reply (2) 29-25. White then sacrifices his three men by 17-14 and after (3) 25-27 (or 9-27) plays 28-32. Black must take the third man, and White recaptures two men by 32-14, pinning both of the remaining black men.

The longest stroke known to have occurred in actual play arose in a game the opening of which went as follows:

Black	White
(1) 12-16	21-17
(2) 16-20	17-13

PROBLEM No. 2—WHITE TO MOVE AND WIN

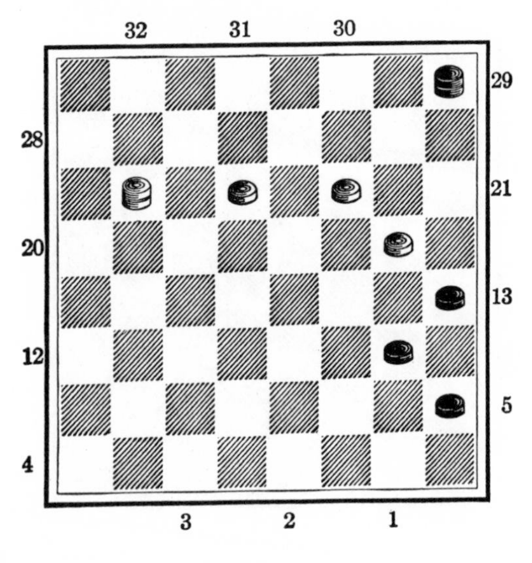

DIAGRAM 117

(3)	10-14	23-19
(4)	14-17	19-16
(5)	17-21	16-12
(6)	11-16	22-18
(7)	8-11	25-22
(8)	7-10	26-23
(9)	10-14	24-19
(10)	14-17	31-26
(11)	4-8	19-15

PROBLEM No. 3—BLACK TO PLAY AND WIN

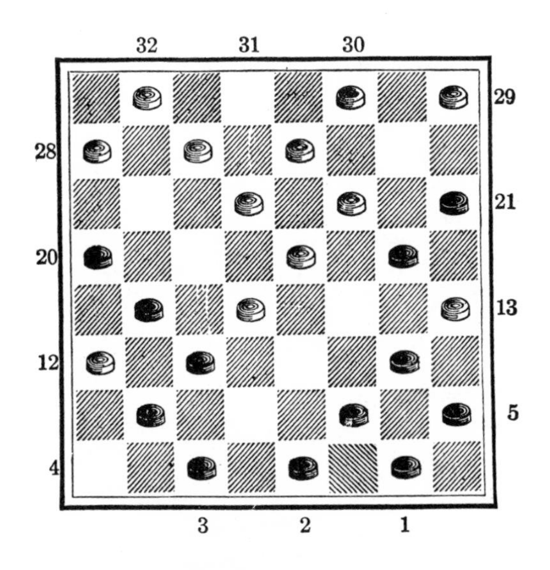

DIAGRAM 118

Now the position of the diagram is reached, in which Black wins by

(12)	21-25	30-14
(13)	16-19	23-7
(14)	3-19	12-3
(15)	19-24	28-19

(16)	2-7	3-10
(17)	6-31	13-6
(18)	1-17	22-13
(19)	31-15	

Completing a stroke, which removes 18 pieces from the board.

(19)	...	32-27
(20)	15-10	29-25
(21)	5-9	

To get the move

(21)	...	13-6
(22)	10-1	25-22
(23)	1-6	22-18
(24)	6-10	27-23
(25)	20-24	23-19
(26)	24-27	18-15
(27)	10-7	19-16
(28)	27-31	15-11
(29)	7-3	16-2
(30)	31-27	11-8
(31)	27-24	8-4
(32)	24-19	4-8
(33)	19-15	8-4
(34)	15-11 and wins.	

CATALOGUE OF DOVER BOOKS

Chess, Checkers, Games, Go

THE ADVENTURE OF CHESS, Edward Lasker. A lively history of chess, from its ancient beginnings in the Indian 4-handed game of Chaturanga, through to the great players of our day, as told by one of America's finest masters. He introduces such unusual sidelights and amusing oddities as Maelzel's chess-playing automaton that beat Napoleon 3 times. Major discussion of chess-playing machines and personal memories of Nimzovich, Capablanca, etc. 5-page chess primer. 11 illustrations, 53 diagrams. 296pp. 5⅜ x 8. S510 Paperbound **$1.75**

A TREASURY OF CHESS LORE, edited by Fred Reinfeld. A delightful collection of anecdotes, short stories, aphorisms by and about the masters, poems, accounts of games and tournaments, photography. Hundreds of humorous, pithy, satirical, wise, and historical episodes, comments, and word portraits. A fascinating "must" for chess players; revealing and perhaps seductive to those who wonder what their friends see in the game. 48 photographs (14 full page plates) 12 diagrams. xi + 306pp. 5⅜ x 8. T458 Paperbound **$1.75**

HOW DO YOU PLAY CHESS? by Fred Reinfeld. A prominent expert covers every basic rule of chess for the beginner in 86 questions and answers: moves, powers of pieces, rationale behind moves, how to play forcefully, history of chess, and much more. Bibliography of chess publications. 11 board diagrams. 48 pages. **FREE**

THE PLEASURES OF CHESS, Assiac. Internationally known British writer, influential chess columnist, writes wittily about wide variety of chess subjects: Anderssen's "Immortal Game;" only game in which both opponents resigned at once; psychological tactics of Reshevsky, Lasker; varieties played by masters for relaxation, such as "losing chess;" sacrificial orgies; etc. These anecdotes, witty observations will give you fresh appreciation of game. 43 problems. 150 diagrams. 139pp. 5⅜ x 8. T597 Paperbound **$1.25**

WIN AT CHESS, F. Reinfeld. 300 practical chess situations from actual tournament play to sharpen your chess eye and test your skill. Traps, sacrifices, mates, winning combinations, subtle exchanges, show you how to WIN AT CHESS. Short notes and tables of solutions and alternative moves help you evaluate your progress. Learn to think ahead playing the "crucial moments" of historic games. 300 diagrams. Notes and solutions. Formerly titled CHESS QUIZ. vi + 120pp. 5⅜ x 8. T438 Paperbound **$1.00**

THE ART OF CHESS, James Mason. An unabridged reprinting of the latest revised edition of the most famous general study of chess ever written. Also included, a complete supplement by Fred Reinfeld, "How Do You Play Chess?", invaluable to beginners for its lively question and answer method. Mason, an early 20th century master, teaches the beginning and intermediate player more than 90 openings, middle game, end game, how to see more moves ahead, to plan purposefully, attack, sacrifice, defend, exchange, and govern general strategy. Supplement. 448 diagrams. 1947 Reinfeld-Bernstein text. Bibliography. xvi + 340pp. 5⅜ x 8. T463 Paperbound **$2.00**

THE PRINCIPLES OF CHESS, James Mason. This "great chess classic" (N. Y. Times) is a general study covering all aspects of the game: basic forces, resistance, obstruction, opposition, relative values, mating, typical end game situations, combinations, much more. The last section discusses openings, with 50 games illustrating modern master play of Rubinstein, Spielmann, Lasker, Capablanca, etc., selected and annotated by Fred Reinfeld. Will improve the game of any intermediate-skilled player, but is so forceful and lucid that an absolute beginner might use it to become an accomplished player. 1946 Reinfeld edition. 166 diagrams. 378pp. 5⅜ x 8. T646 Paperbound **$1.85**

LASKER'S MANUAL OF CHESS, Dr. Emanuel Lasker. Probably the greatest chess player of modern times, Dr. Emanuel Lasker held the world championship 28 years, independent of passing schools or fashions. This unmatched study of the game, chiefly for intermediate to skilled players, analyzes basic methods, combinations, position play, the aesthetics of chess, dozens of different openings, etc., with constant reference to great modern games. Contains a brilliant exposition of Steinitz's important theories. Introduction by Fred Reinfeld. Tables of Lasker's tournament record. 3 indices. 308 diagrams. 1 photograph. xxx + 349pp. 5⅜ x 8. T640 Paperbound **$2.25**

THE ART OF CHESS COMBINATION, E. Znosko-Borovsky. Proves that combinations, perhaps the most aesthetically satisfying, successful technique in chess, can be an integral part of your game, instead of a haphazard occurrence. Games of Capablanca, Rubinstein, Nimzovich, Bird, etc. grouped according to common features, perceptively analyzed to show that every combination begins in certain simple ideas. Will help you to plan many moves ahead. Technical terms almost completely avoided. "In the teaching of chess he may claim to have no superior," P. W. Sergeant. Introduction. Exercises. Solutions. Index. 223pp. 5⅜ x 8. T583 Paperbound **$1.60**

MODERN IDEAS IN CHESS, Richard Reti. An enduring classic, because of its unrivalled explanation of the way master chess had developed in the past hundred years. Reti, who was an outstanding theoretician and player, explains each advance in chess by concentrating on the games of the single master most closely associated with it: Morphy, Anderssen, Steinitz, Lasker, Alekhine, other world champions. Play the games in this volume, study Reti's perceptive observations, and have a living picture of the road chess has travelled. Introduction. 34 diagrams. 192pp. 5⅜ x 8. T638 Paperbound **$1.25**

THE BOOK OF THE NEW YORK INTERNATIONAL CHESS TOURNAMENT, 1924, annotated by A. Alekhine and edited by H. Helms. Long a rare collector's item, this is the book of one of the most brilliant tournaments of all time, during which Capablanca, Lasker, Alekhine, Reti, and others immeasurably enriched chess theory in a thrilling contest. All 110 games played, with Alekhine's unusually penetrating notes. 15 photographs. xi + 271pp. 5⅜ x 8. T752 Paperbound **$1.85**

KERES' BEST GAMES OF CHESS, selected, annotated by F. Reinfeld. 90 best games, 1931-1948, by one of boldest, most exciting players of modern chess. Games against Alekhine, Bogolyubov, Capablanca, Euwe, Fine, Reshevsky, other masters, show his treatments of openings such as Giuoco Piano, Alekhine Defense, Queen's Gambit Declined; attacks, sacrifices, alternative methods. Preface by Keres gives personal glimpses, evaluations of rivals. 110 diagrams. 272pp. 5⅜ x 8. T593 Paperbound **$1.35**

HYPERMODERN CHESS as developed in the games of its greatest exponent, ARON NIMZOVICH, edited by Fred Reinfeld. An intensely original player and analyst, Nimzovich's extraordinary approaches startled and often angered the chess world. This volume, designed for the average player, shows in his victories over Alekhine, Lasker, Marshall, Rubinstein, Spielmann, and others, how his iconoclastic methods infused new life into the game. Use Nimzovich to invigorate your play and startle opponents. Introduction. Indices of players and openings. 180 diagrams. viii + 220pp. 5⅜ x 8. T448 Paperbound **$1.50**

THE DEVELOPMENT OF A CHESS GENIUS: 100 INSTRUCTIVE GAMES OF ALEKHINE, F. Reinfeld. 100 games of the chess giant's formative years, 1905-1914, from age 13 to maturity, each annotated and commented upon by Fred Reinfeld. Included are matches against Bogolyubov, Capablanca, Tarrasch, and many others. You see the growth of an inexperienced genius into one of the greatest players of all time. Many of these games have never appeared before in book form. "One of America's most significant contributions to the chess world," Chess Life. New introduction. Index of players, openings. 204 illustrations. xv +227pp. 5¾ x 8. T551 Paperbound **$1.35**

RESHEVSKY'S BEST GAMES OF CHESS, Samuel Reshevsky. One time 4-year-old chess genius, 5-time winner U. S. Chess Championship, selects, annotates 110 of his best games, illustrating theories, favorite methods of play against Capablanca, Alekhine, Bogolyubov, Kashdan, Vidmar, Botvinnik, others. Clear, non-technical style. Personal impressions of opponents, autobiographical material, tournament match record. Formerly "Reshevsky on Chess." 309 diagrams, 2 photos. 288pp. 5⅜ x 8. T606 Paperbound **$1.25**

ONE HUNDRED SELECTED GAMES, Mikhail Botvinnik. Author's own choice of his best games before becoming World Champion in 1948, beginning with first big tournament, the USSR Championship, 1927. Shows his great power of analysis as he annotates these games, giving strategy, technique against Alekhine, Capablanca, Euwe, Keres, Reshevsky, Smyslov, Vidmar, many others. Discusses his career, methods of play, system of training. 6 studies of endgame positions. 221 diagrams. 272pp. 5⅜ x 8. T620 Paperbound **$1.50**

RUBINSTEIN'S CHESS MASTERPIECES, selected, annotated by Hans Kmoch. Thoroughgoing mastery of opening, middle game; faultless technique in endgame, particularly rook and pawn endings; ability to switch from careful positional play to daring combinations; all distinguish the play of Rubinstein. 100 best games, against Janowski, Nimzowitch, Tarrasch, Vidmar, Capablanca, other greats, carefully annotated, will improve your game rapidly. Biographical introduction, B. F. Winkelman. 103 diagrams. 192pp. 5⅜ x 8. T617 Paperbound **$1.25**

TARRASCH'S BEST GAMES OF CHESS, selected & annotated by Fred Reinfeld. First definitive collection of games by Siegbert Tarrasch, winner of 7 international tournaments, and the leading theorist of classical chess. 183 games cover fifty years of play against Mason, Mieses, Paulsen, Teichmann, Pillsbury, Janwoski, others. Reinfeld includes Tarrasch's own analyses of many of these games. A careful study and replaying of the games will give you a sound understanding of classical methods, and many hours of enjoyment. Introduction. Indexes. 183 diagrams. xxiv + 386pp. 5⅜ x 8. T644 Paperbound **$2.00**

MARSHALL'S BEST GAMES OF CHESS, F. J. Marshall. Grandmaster, U. S. Champion for 27 years, tells story of career; presents magnificent collection of 140 of best games, annotated by himself. Games against Alekhine, Capablanca, Emanuel Lasker, Janowski, Rubinstein, Pillsbury, etc. Special section analyzes openings such as King's Gambit, Ruy Lopez, Alekhine's Defense, Giuoco Piano, others. A study of Marshall's brilliant offensives, slashing attacks, extraordinary sacrifices, will rapidly improve your game. Formerly "My Fifty Years of Chess." Introduction. 19 diagrams. 13 photos. 250pp. 5⅜ x 8. T604 Paperbound **$1.45**

THE HASTINGS CHESS TOURNAMENT, 1895, edited by Horace F. Cheshire. This is the complete tournament book of the famous Hastings 1895 tournament. One of the most exciting tournaments ever to take place, it evoked the finest play from such players as Dr. Lasker, Steinitz, Tarrasch, Harry Pillsbury, Mason, Tchigorin, Schlecter, and others. It was not only extremely exciting as an event, it also created first-rate chess. This book contains fully annotated all 230 games, full information about the playing events, biographies of the players, and much other material that makes it a chess classic. 22 photos, 174 diagrams. x + 370pp. 5⅝ x 8½. T288 Paperbound **$2.00**

THE BOOK OF THE NOTTINGHAM INTERNATIONAL CHESS TOURNAMENT, 1936, Annotated by Dr. Alexander Alekhine. The Nottingham 1936 tournament is regarded by many chess enthusiasts as the greatest tournament of recent years. It brought together all the living former world champions, the current chess champion, and the future world champion: Dr. Lasker, Capablanca, Alekhine, Euwe, Botvinnik, and Reshevsky, Fine, Flohr, Tartakover, Vidmar, and Bogoljubov. The play was brilliant throughout. This volume contains all 105 of the games played, provided with the remarkable annotations of Alekhine. 1 illustration, 121 diagrams. xx + 291pp. 5⅜ x 8½. T189 Paperbound **$2.00**

CHESS FOR FUN AND CHESS FOR BLOOD, Edward Lasker. A genial, informative book by one of century's leading masters. Incisive comments on chess as a form of art and recreation, on how a master prepares for and plays a tournament. Best of all is author's move-by-move analysis of his game with Dr. Emanuel Lasker in 1924 World Tournament, a charming and thorough recreation of one of the great games in history: the author's mental processes; how his calculations were upset; how both players blundered; the surprising outcome. Who could not profit from this study-in-depth? For the enthusiast who likes to read about chess as well as play it. Corrected (1942) edition. Preface contains 8 letters to author about the fun of chess. 95 illustrations by Maximilian Mopp. 224pp. 5⅜ x 8½. T146 Paperbound **$1.25**

HOW NOT TO PLAY CHESS, Eugene A. Znosko-Borovsky. Sticking to a few well-chosen examples and explaining every step along the way, an outstanding chess expositor shows how to avoid playing a hit-or-miss game and instead develop general plans of action based on positional analysis: weak and strong squares, the notion of the controlled square, how to seize control of open lines, weak points in the pawn structure, and so on. Definition and illustration of typical chess mistakes plus 20 problems (from master games) added by Fred Reinfeld for the 1949 edition and a number of good-to-memorize tips make this a lucid book that can teach in a few hours what might otherwise take years to learn. 119pp. 5⅜ x 8.
T920 Paperbound **$1.00**

THE SOVIET SCHOOL OF CHESS, A. Kotov and M. Yudovich. 128 master games, most unavailable elsewhere, by 51 outstanding players, including Botvinnik, Keres, Smyslov, Tal, against players like Capablanca, Euwe, Reshevsky. All carefully annotated, analyzed. Valuable biographical information about each player, early history of Russian chess, careers and contributions of Chigorin and Alekhine, development of Soviet school from 1920 to present with full over-all study of main features of its games, history of Russian chess literature. The most comprehensive work on Russian chess ever printed, the richest single sourcebook for up-to-date Russian theory and strategy. New introduction. Appendix of Russian Grandmasters, Masters, Master Composers. Two indexes (Players, Games). 30 photographs. 182 diagrams. vi + 390pp. 5⅜ x 8. T26 Paperbound **$2.00**

THE ART OF THE CHECKMATE, Georges Renaud and Victor Kahn. Two former national chess champions of France examine 127 games, identify 23 kinds of mate, and show the rationale for each. These include Legal's pseudo sacrifice, the double check, the smothered mate, Greco's mate, Morphy's mate, the mate of two bishops, two knights, many, many more. Analysis of ideas, not memorization problems. Review quizzes with answers help readers gauge progress. 80 quiz examples and solutions. 299 diagrams. vi + 208pp.
T106 Paperbound **$1.50**

HOW TO SOLVE CHESS PROBLEMS, K. S. Howard. Full of practical suggestions for the fan or the beginner—who knows only the moves of the chessmen. Contains preliminary section and 58 two-move, 46 three-move, and 8 four-move problems composed by 27 outstanding American problem creators in the last 30 years. Explanation of all terms and exhaustive index. "Just what is wanted for the student," Brian Harley. 112 problems, solutions. vi +171pp. 5⅜ x 8.
T748 Paperbound **$1.25**

CHESS STRATEGY, Edward Lasker. Keres, Fine, and other great players have acknowledged their debt to this book, which has taught just about the whole modern school how to play forcefully and intelligently. Covers fundamentals, general strategic principles, middle and end game, objects of attack, etc. Includes 48 dramatic games from master tournaments, all fully analyzed. "Best textbook I know in English," J. R. Capablanca. New introduction by author. Table of openings. Index. 167 illustrations. vii + 282pp. 5⅜ x 8.
T528 Paperbound **$1.65**

REINFELD ON THE END GAME IN CHESS, F. Reinfeld. Formerly titled PRACTICAL END-GAME PLAY, this book contains clear, simple analyses of 62 end games by such masters as Alekhine, Tarrasch, Marshall, Morphy, Capablanca, and many others. Primary emphasis is on the general principles of transition from middle play to end play. This book is unusual in analyzing weak or incorrect moves to show how error occurs and how to avoid it. Covers king and pawn, minor piece, queen endings, weak squares, centralization, tempo moves, and many other vital factors. 62 diagrams. vi + 177pp. 5⅜ x 8. T417 Paperbound **$1.25**

THE AMERICAN TWO-MOVE CHESS PROBLEM, Kenneth S. Howard. One of this country's foremost contemporary problem composers selects an interesting, diversified collection of the best two-movers by 58 top American composers. Involving complete blocks, mutates, line openings and closings, other unusual moves, these problems will help almost any player improve his strategic approach. Probably has no equal for all around artistic excellence, surprising keymoves, interesting strategy. Includes 30-page history of development of American two-mover from Loyd, its founder, to the present. Index of composers. vii + 99pp. 5⅜ x 8½.
T997 Paperbound **$1.00**

WIN AT CHECKERS, M. Hopper. (Formerly CHECKERS). The former World's Unrestricted Checker Champion discusses the principles cf the game, expert's shots and traps, problems for the beginner, standard openings, locating your best move, the end game, opening "blitzkrieg" moves, ways to draw when you are behind your opponent, etc. More than 100 detailed questions and answers anticipate your problems. Appendix. 75 problems with solutions and diagrams. Index. 79 figures. xi + 107pp. 5⅜ x 8. T363 Paperbound **$1.00**

GAMES ANCIENT AND ORIENTAL, AND HOW TO PLAY THEM, E. Falkener. A connoisseur's selection of exciting and different games: Oriental varieties of chess, with unusual pieces and moves (including Japanese shogi); the original pachisi; go; reconstructions of lost Roman and Egyptian games; and many more. Full rules and sample games. Now play at home the games that have entertained millions, not on a fad basis, but for millennia. 345 illustrations and figures. iv + 366pp. 5⅜ x 8. T739 Paperbound **$2.00**

GO AND GO-MOKU, Edward Lasker. A fascinating Oriental game, Go, is winning new devotees in America daily. Rules that you can learn in a few minutes—a wealth of combinations that makes it more profound than chess! This is an easily followed step-by-step explanation of this 2000-year-old game, beginning with fundamentals. New chapter on advanced strategy in this edition! Also contains rules for Go-Moku, a very easy sister game. 72 diagrams. xix + 215pp. 5⅜ x 8. T613 Paperbound **$1.50**

HOW TO FORCE CHECKMATE, F. Reinfeld. Formerly titled CHALLENGE TO CHESSPLAYERS, this is an invaluable collection of 300 lightning strokes selected from actual masters' play, which will demonstrate how to smash your opponent's game with strong decisive moves. No board needed — clear, practical diagrams and easy-to-understand solutions. Learn to plan up to three moves ahead and play a superior end game. 300 diagrams. 111pp. 5⅜ x 8.
T439 Paperbound **$1.35**

CHESSBOARD MAGIC! A COLLECTION OF 160 BRILLIANT ENDINGS, I. Chernev. Contains 160 endgame compositions, all illustrating not only ingenuity of composition, but inherent beauty of solution. In one, five Knights are needed to force mate; in another White forces stalemate though Black finishes eight passed pawns ahead; 150 more, all remarkable, all will sharpen your imagination and increase your skill. "Inexhaustible source of entertainment, an endless feast of delight," Reuben Fine, Grandmaster. Introduction. 160 diagrams. Index of composers. vii + 172pp. 5⅜ x 8. T607 Paperbound **$1.00**

LEARN CHESS FROM THE MASTERS, F. Reinfeld. Formerly titled CHESS BY YOURSELF, this book contains 10 games which you play against such masters as Marshall, Bronstein, Najdorf, and others, and an easy system for grading each move you make against a variety of other possible moves. Detailed annotations reveal the principles of the game through actual play. 91 diagrams. viii + 144pp. 5⅜ x 8. T362 Paperbound **$1.25**

MORPHY'S GAMES OF CHESS, edited by Philip W. Sergeant. You can put boldness into your game by following the brilliant, forceful moves of the man who has been called the greatest chess player of all time. Here are 300 of Morphy's best games carefully annotated to reveal Morphy's principles. 54 classics against masters like Anderssen, Harrwitz, Bird, Paulsen, and others. 52 games at odds; 54 blindfold games; plus over 100 others. Unabridged reissue of the latest revised edition. Bibliography. New introduction by Fred Reinfeld. Annotations and introduction by Sergeant. Index. 235 diagrams. x + 352pp. 5⅜ x 8. T386 Paperbound **$2.00**

CHESS PRAXIS, Aron Nimzovich. Nimzovich was the stormy petrel of chess in the first decades of this century, and his system, known as hypermodern chess, revolutionized all play since his time. Casting aside the classical chess theory of Steinitz and Tarrasch, he created his own analysis of chess, considering dynamic patterns as they emerge during play. This is the fullest exposition of his ideas, and it is easily one of the dozen greatest books ever written on chess. Nimzovich illustrates each of his principles with at least two games, and shows how he applied his concepts successfully in games against such masters as Alekhine, Tarrasch, Reti, Rubinstein, Capablanca, Spielmann and others. Indispensable to every serious chess player. Translated by J. DuMont. 135 diagrams, 1 photo. xi + 364pp. 5½ x 8⅝.
T296 Paperbound **$2.25**

CHESS AND CHECKERS: THE WAY TO MASTERSHIP, Edward Lasker. Complete, lucid instructions for the beginner—and valuable suggestions for the advanced player! For both games the great master and teacher presents fundamentals, elementary tactics, and steps toward becoming a superior player. He concentrates on general principles rather than a mass of rules, comprehension rather than brute memory. Historical introduction. 118 diagrams. xiv + 167pp. 5⅜ x 8. T657 Paperbound **$1.15**

Social Sciences

SOCIAL THOUGHT FROM LORE TO SCIENCE, H. E. Barnes and H. Becker. An immense survey of sociological thought and ways of viewing, studying, planning, and reforming society from earliest times to the present. Includes thought on society of preliterate peoples, ancient non-Western cultures, and every great movement in Europe, America, and modern Japan. Analyzes hundreds of great thinkers: Plato, Augustine, Bodin, Vico, Montesquieu, Herder, Comte, Marx, etc. Weighs the contributions of utopians, sophists, fascists and communists; economists, jurists, philosophers, ecclesiastics, and every 19th and 20th century school of scientific sociology, anthropology, and social psychology throughout the world. Combines topical, chronological, and regional approaches, treating the evolution of social thought as a process rather than as a series of mere topics. "Impressive accuracy, competence, and discrimination . . . easily the best single survey," Nation. Thoroughly revised, with new material up to 1960. 2 indexes. Over 2200 bibliographical notes. Three volume set. Total of 1586pp. 5⅜ x 8.
T901 Vol I Paperbound **$2.50**
T902 Vol II Paperbound **$2.50**
T903 Vol III Paperbound **$2.50**
The set **$7.50**

FOLKWAYS, William Graham Sumner. A classic of sociology, a searching and thorough examination of patterns of behaviour from primitive, ancient Greek and Judaic, Medieval Christian, African, Oriental, Melanesian, Australian, Islamic, to modern Western societies. Thousands of illustrations of social, sexual, and religious customs, mores, laws, and institutions. Hundreds of categories: Labor, Wealth, Abortion, Primitive Justice, Life Policy, Slavery, Cannibalism, Uncleanness and the Evil Eye, etc. Will extend the horizon of every reader by showing the relativism of his own culture. Prefatory note by A. G. Keller. Introduction by William Lyon Phelps. Bibliography. Index. xiii + 692pp. 5⅜ x 8. T508 Paperbound **$2.49**

PRIMITIVE RELIGION, P. Radin. A thorough treatment by a noted anthropologist of the nature and origin of man's belief in the supernatural and the influences that have shaped religious expression in primitive societies. Ranging from the Arunta, Ashanti, Aztec, Bushman, Crow, Fijian, etc., of Africa, Australia, Pacific Islands, the Arctic, North and South America, Prof. Radin integrates modern psychology, comparative religion, and economic thought with first-hand accounts gathered by himself and other scholars of primitive initiations, training of the shaman, and other fascinating topics. "Excellent," NATURE (London). Unabridged reissue of 1st edition. New author's preface. Bibliographic notes. Index. x + 322pp. 5⅜ x 8.
T393 Paperbound **$2.00**

PRIMITIVE MAN AS PHILOSOPHER, P. Radin. A standard anthropological work covering primitive thought on such topics as the purpose of life, marital relations, freedom of thought, symbolism, death, resignation, the nature of reality, personality, gods, and many others. Drawn from factual material gathered from the Winnebago, Oglala Sioux, Maori, Baganda, Batak, Zuni, among others, it does not distort ideas by removing them from context but interprets strictly within the original framework. Extensive selections of original primitive documents. Bibliography. Index. xviii + 402pp. 5⅜ x 8. T392 Paperbound **$2.25**

A TREATISE ON SOCIOLOGY, THE MIND AND SOCIETY, Vilfredo Pareto. This treatise on human society is one of the great classics of modern sociology. First published in 1916, its careful catalogue of the innumerable manifestations of non-logical human conduct (Book One); the theory of "residues," leading to the premise that sentiment not logic determines human behavior (Book Two), and of "derivations," beliefs derived from desires (Book Three); and the general description of society made up of non-elite and elite, consisting of "foxes" who live by cunning and "lions" who live by force, stirred great controversy. But Pareto's passion for isolation and classification of elements and factors, and his allegiance to scientific method as the key tool for scrutinizing the human situation made his a truly twentieth-century mind and his work a catalytic influence on certain later social commentators. These four volumes (bound as two) require no special training to be appreciated and any reader who wishes to gain a complete understanding of modern sociological theory, regardless of special field of interest, will find them a must. Reprint of revised (corrected) printing of original edition. Translated by Andrew Bongiorno and Arthur Livingston. Index. Bibliography. Appendix containing index-summary of theorems. 48 diagrams. Four volumes bound as two. Total of 2063pp. 5⅜ x 8½. The set Clothbound **$15.00**

THE POLISH PEASANT IN EUROPE AND AMERICA, William I. Thomas, Florian Znaniecki. A seminal sociological study of peasant primary groups (family and community) and the disruptions produced by a new industrial system and immigration to America. The peasant's family, class system, religious and aesthetic attitudes, and economic life are minutely examined and analyzed in hundreds of pages of primary documentation, particularly letters between family members. The disorientation caused by new environments is scrutinized in detail (a 312-page autobiography of an immigrant is especially valuable and revealing) in an attempt to find common experiences and reactions. The famous "Methodological Note" sets forth the principles which guided the authors. When out of print this set has sold for as much as $50. 2nd revised edition. 2 vols. Vol. 1: xv + 1115pp. Vol. 2: 1135pp. Index. 6 x 9.
T478 Clothbound 2 vol. set **$12.50**

Fiction

FLATLAND, E. A. Abbott. A science-fiction classic of life in a 2-dimensional world that is also a first-rate introduction to such aspects of modern science as relativity and hyperspace. Political, moral, satirical, and humorous overtones have made FLATLAND fascinating reading for thousands. 7th edition. New introduction by Banesh Hoffmann. 16 illustrations. 128pp. 5⅜ x 8. T1 Paperbound **$1.00**

THE WONDERFUL WIZARD OF OZ, L. F. Baum. Only edition in print with all the original W. W. Denslow illustrations in full color—as much a part of "The Wizard" as Tenniel's drawings are of "Alice in Wonderland." "The Wizard" is still America's best-loved fairy tale, in which, as the author expresses it, "The wonderment and joy are retained and the heartaches and nightmares left out." Now today's young readers can enjoy every word and wonderful picture of the original book. New introduction by Martin Gardner. A Baum bibliography. 23 full-page color plates. viii + 268pp. 5⅜ x 8. T691 Paperbound **$1.50**

THE MARVELOUS LAND OF OZ, L. F. Baum. This is the equally enchanting sequel to the "Wizard," continuing the adventures of the Scarecrow and the Tin Woodman. The hero this time is a little boy named Tip, and all the delightful Oz magic is still present. This is the Oz book with the Animated Saw-Horse, the Woggle-Bug, and Jack Pumpkinhead. All the original John R. Neill illustrations, 10 in full color. 287 pp. 5⅜ x 8. T692 Paperbound **$1.50**

28 SCIENCE FICTION STORIES OF H. G. WELLS. Two full unabridged novels, MEN LIKE GODS and STAR BEGOTTEN, plus 26 short stories by the master science-fiction writer of all time! Stories of space, time, invention, exploration, future adventure—an indispensable part of the library of everyone interested in science and adventure. PARTIAL CONTENTS: Men Like Gods, The Country of the Blind, In the Abyss, The Crystal Egg, The Man Who Could Work Miracles, A Story of the Days to Come, The Valley of Spiders, and 21 more! 928pp. 5⅜ x 8.
T265 Clothbound **$4.50**

THREE MARTIAN NOVELS, Edgar Rice Burroughs. Contains: Thuvia, Maid of Mars; The Chessmen of Mars; and The Master Mind of Mars. High adventure set in an imaginative and intricate conception of the Red Planet. Mars is peopled with an intelligent, heroic human race which lives in densely populated cities and with fierce barbarians who inhabit dead sea bottoms. Other exciting creatures abound amidst an inventive framework of Martian history and geography. Complete unabridged reprintings of the first edition. 16 illustrations by J. Allen St. John. vi + 499pp. 5⅜ x 8½. T39 Paperbound **$1.85**

SEVEN SCIENCE FICTION NOVELS, H. G. Wells. Full unabridged texts of 7 science-fiction novels of the master. Ranging from biology, physics, chemistry, astronomy to sociology and other studies, Mr. Wells extrapolates whole worlds of strange and intriguing character. "One will have to go far to match this for entertainment, excitement, and sheer pleasure . . . ," NEW YORK TIMES. Contents: The Time Machine, The Island of Dr. Moreau, First Men in the Moon, The Invisible Man, The War of the Worlds, The Food of the Gods, In the Days of the Comet. 1015pp. 5⅜ x 8. T264 Clothbound **$4.50**

THE LAND THAT TIME FORGOT and THE MOON MAID, Edgar Rice Burroughs. In the opinion of many, Burroughs' best work. The first concerns a strange island where evolution is individual rather than phylogenetic. Speechless anthropoids develop into intelligent human beings within a single generation. The second projects the reader far into the future and describes the first voyage to the Moon (in the year 2025), the conquest of the Earth by the Moon, and years of violence and adventure as the enslaved Earthmen try to regain possession of their planet. "An imaginative tour de force that keeps the reader keyed up and expectant," NEW YORK TIMES. Complete, unabridged text of the original two novels (three parts in each). 5 illustrations by J. Allen St. John. vi + 552pp. 5⅜ x 8½.
T1020 Clothbound **$3.75**
T358 Paperbound **$2.00**

3 ADVENTURE NOVELS by H. Rider Haggard. Complete texts of "She," "King Solomon's Mines," "Allan Quatermain." Qualities of discovery; desire for immortality; search for primitive, for what is unadorned by civilization, have kept these novels of African adventure exciting, alive to readers from R. L. Stevenson to George Orwell. 636pp. 5⅜ x 8.
T584 Paperbound **$2.00**

A PRINCESS OF MARS and A FIGHTING MAN OF MARS: TWO MARTIAN NOVELS BY EDGAR RICE BURROUGHS. "Princess of Mars" is the very first of the great Martian novels written by Burroughs, and it is probably the best of them all; it set the pattern for all of his later fantasy novels and contains a thrilling cast of strange peoples and creatures and the formula of Olympian heroism amidst ever-fluctuating fortunes which Burroughs carries off so successfully. "Fighting Man" returns to the same scenes and cities—many years later. A mad scientist, a degenerate dictator, and an indomitable defender of the right clash—with the fate of the Red Planet at stake! Complete, unabridged reprinting of original editions. Illustrations by F. E. Schoonover and Hugh Hutton. v + 356pp. 5⅜ x 8½.
T1140 Paperbound **$1.75**

THE PIRATES OF VENUS and LOST ON VENUS: TWO VENUS NOVELS BY EDGAR RICE BURROUGHS. Two related novels, complete and unabridged. Exciting adventure on the planet Venus with Earthman Carson Napier broken-field running through one dangerous episode after another. All lovers of swashbuckling science fiction will enjoy these two stories set in a world of fascinating societies, fierce beasts, 5000-ft. trees, lush vegetation, and wide seas. Illustrations by Fortunino Matania. Total of vi + 340pp. 5⅜ x 8½. T1053 Paperbound **$1.75**

RURITANIA COMPLETE: THE PRISONER OF ZENDA and RUPERT OF HENTZAU, Anthony Hope. The first edition to include in one volume both the continually-popular "Prisoner of Zenda" and its equally-absorbing sequel. Hope's mythical country of Ruritania has become a household word and the activities of its inhabitants almost a common heritage. Unabridged reprinting. 14 illustrations by Charles Dana Gibson. vi + 414pp. 5⅜ x 8. T69 Paperbound **$1.35**

GHOST AND HORROR STORIES OF AMBROSE BIERCE, Selected and introduced by E. F. Bleiler. 24 morbid, eerie tales—the cream of Bierce's fiction output. Contains such memorable pieces as "The Moonlit Road," "The Damned Thing," "An Inhabitant of Carcosa," "The Eyes of the Panther," "The Famous Gilson Bequest," "The Middle Toe of the Right Foot," and other chilling stories, plus the essay, "Visions of the Night" in which Bierce gives us a kind of rationale for his aesthetic of horror. New collection (1964). xxii + 199pp. 5⅜ x 8⅜. T767 Paperbound **$1.00**

BEST GHOST STORIES OF J. S. LE FANU, Selected and introduced by E. F. Bleiler. LeFanu is deemed the greatest name in Victorian supernatural fiction. Here are 16 of his best horror stories, including 2 nouvelles: "Carmilla," a classic vampire tale couched in a perverse eroticism, and "The Haunted Baronet." Also: "Sir Toby's Will," "Green Tea," "Schalken the Painter," "Ultor de Lacy," "The Familiar," etc. The first American publication of about half of this material: a long-overdue opportunity to get a choice sampling of LeFanu's work. New selection (1964). 8 illustrations. 5⅜ x 8⅜. T415 Paperbound **$1.85**

FIVE GREAT DOG NOVELS, edited by Blanche Cirker. The complete original texts of five classic dog novels that have delighted and thrilled millions of children and adults throughout the world with stories of loyalty, adventure, and courage. Full texts of Jack London's "The Call of the Wild"; John Brown's "Rab and His Friends"; Alfred Ollivant's "Bob, Son of Battle"; Marshall Saunders' "Beautiful Joe"; and Ouida's "A Dog of Flanders." 21 illustrations from the original editions. 495pp. 5⅜ x 8. T777 Paperbound **$1.75**

THE CASTING AWAY OF MRS. LECKS AND MRS. ALESHINE, F. R. Stockton. A charming light novel by Frank Stockton, one of America's finest humorists (and author of "The Lady, or the Tiger?"). This book has made millions of Americans laugh at the reflection of themselves in two middle-aged American women involved in some of the strangest adventures on record. You will laugh, too, as they endure shipwreck, desert island, and blizzard with maddening tranquility. Also contains complete text of "The Dusantes," sequel to "The Casting Away." 49 original illustrations by F. D. Steele. vii + 142pp. 5⅜ x 8. T743 Paperbound **$1.00**

AT THE EARTH'S CORE, PELLUCIDAR, TANAR OF PELLUCIDAR: THREE SCIENCE FICTION NOVELS BY EDGAR RICE BURROUGHS. Complete, unabridged texts of the first three Pellucidar novels. Tales of derring-do by the famous master of science fiction. The locale for these three related stories is the inner surface of the hollow Earth where we discover the world of Pellucidar, complete with all types of bizarre, menacing creatures, strange peoples, and alluring maidens—guaranteed to delight all Burroughs fans and a wide circle of advenutre lovers. Illustrated by J. Allen St. John and P. F. Berdanier. vi + 433pp. 5⅜ x 8½. T1051 Paperbound **$2.00**

THE WAR IN THE AIR, IN THE DAYS OF THE COMET, THE FOOD OF THE GODS: THREE SCIENCE FICTION NOVELS BY H. G. WELLS. Three exciting Wells offerings bearing on vital social and philosophical issues of his and our own day. Here are tales of air power, strategic bombing, East vs. West, the potential miracles of science, the potential disasters from outer space, the relationship between scientific advancement and moral progress, etc. First reprinting of "War in the Air" in almost 50 years. An excellent sampling of Wells at his storytelling best. Complete, unabridged reprintings. 16 illustrations. 645pp. 5⅜ x 8½. T1135 Paperbound **$2.00**

DAVID HARUM, E. N. Westcott. This novel of one of the most lovable, humorous characters in American literature is a prime example of regional humor. It continues to delight people who like their humor dry, their characters quaint, and their plots ingenuous. First book edition to contain complete novel plus chapter found after author's death. Illustrations from first illustrated edition. 192pp. 5⅜ x 8. T580 Paperbound **$1.15**

TO THE SUN? and OFF ON A COMET!, Jules Verne. Complete texts of two of the most imaginative flights into fancy in world literature display the high adventure that have kept Verne's novels read for nearly a century. Only unabridged edition of the best translation, by Edward Roth. Large, easily readable type. 50 illustrations selected from first editions. 462pp. 5⅜ x 8. T634 Paperbound **$1.75**